DELIBERATE PRACTICE IN
CAREER COUNSELING

Essentials of Deliberate Practice Series
Tony Rousmaniere and Alexandre Vaz, Series Editors

Deliberate Practice in Accelerated Experiential Dynamic Psychotherapy
  Natasha C. N. Prenn, Hanna Levenson, Alexandre Vaz, and Tony Rousmaniere

Deliberate Practice in Career Counseling
  Jennifer M. Taylor, Alexandre Vaz, and Tony Rousmaniere

Deliberate Practice in Child and Adolescent Psychotherapy
  Jordan Bate, Tracy A. Prout, Tony Rousmaniere, and Alexandre Vaz

Deliberate Practice in Cognitive Behavioral Therapy
  James F. Boswell and Michael J. Constantino

Deliberate Practice in Dialectical Behavior Therapy
  Tali Boritz, Shelley McMain, Alexandre Vaz, and Tony Rousmaniere

Deliberate Practice in Emotion-Focused Therapy
  Rhonda N. Goldman, Alexandre Vaz, and Tony Rousmaniere

Deliberate Practice in Emotionally Focused Couple Therapy
  Hanna Levenson, Sam Jinich, Alexandre Vaz, and Tony Rousmaniere

Deliberate Practice in Interpersonal Psychotherapy
  Olga Belik, Scott Fairhurst, Jessica M. Schultz, Scott Stuart, Alexandre Vaz, and Tony Rousmaniere

Deliberate Practice in Motivational Interviewing
  Jennifer K. Manuel, Denise Ernst, Alexandre Vaz, and Tony Rousmaniere

Deliberate Practice in Multicultural Therapy
  Jordan Harris, Joel Jin, Sophia Hoffman, Selina Phan, Tracy A. Prout, Tony Rousmaniere, and Alexandre Vaz

Deliberate Practice in Psychedelic-Assisted Therapy
  Shannon Dames, Andrew Penn, Monnica Williams, Joseph A. Zamaria, Tony Rousmaniere, and Alexandre Vaz

Deliberate Practice in Psychodynamic Psychotherapy
  Hanna Levenson, Volney Gay, and Jeffrey L. Binder

Deliberate Practice in Rational Emotive Behavior Therapy
  Mark D. Terjesen, Kristene A. Doyle, Raymond A. DiGiuseppe, Alexandre Vaz, and Tony Rousmaniere

Deliberate Practice in Schema Therapy
  Wendy T. Behary, Joan M. Farrell, Alexandre Vaz, and Tony Rousmaniere

Deliberate Practice in Systemic Family Therapy
  Adrian J. Blow, Ryan B. Seedall, Debra L. Miller, Tony Rousmaniere, and Alexandre Vaz

ESSENTIALS OF DELIBERATE PRACTICE SERIES
TONY ROUSMANIERE AND ALEXANDRE VAZ, SERIES EDITORS

DELIBERATE PRACTICE IN CAREER COUNSELING

JENNIFER M. TAYLOR

ALEXANDRE VAZ

TONY ROUSMANIERE

AMERICAN PSYCHOLOGICAL ASSOCIATION

Copyright © 2025 by the American Psychological Association. All rights, including for text and data mining, AI training, and similar technologies, are reserved. Except as permitted under the United States Copyright Act of 1976, no part of this publication may be reproduced or distributed in any form or by any means, including, but not limited to, the process of scanning and digitization, or stored in a database or retrieval system, without the prior written permission of the publisher.

The opinions and statements published are those of the Authors, and do not necessarily represent the policies of the American Psychological Association. The information contained in this work does not constitute personalized therapeutic advice. Users seeking medical advice, diagnoses, or treatment should consult a medical professional or health care provider. The Authors have worked to ensure that all information in this book is accurate at the time of publication and consistent with general mental health care standards.

Published by
American Psychological Association
750 First Street, NE
Washington, DC 20002
https://www.apa.org

Order Department
https://www.apa.org/pubs/books
order@apa.org

Typeset in Cera Pro by Circle Graphics, Inc., Reisterstown, MD

Printer: Gasch Printing, Odenton, MD
Cover Designer: Mark Karis

Library of Congress Cataloging-in-Publication Data

Names: Taylor, Jennifer M., author. | Vaz, Alexandre, author. | Rousmaniere, Tony, author.
Title: Deliberate practice in career counseling / by Jennifer M. Taylor, Alexandre Vaz, and Tony Rousmaniere.
Description: Washington, DC : American Psychological Association, [2025] | Series: Essentials of deliberate practice series | Includes bibliographical references and index.
Identifiers: LCCN 2024036351 (print) | LCCN 2024036352 (ebook) | ISBN 9781433842887 (paperback) | ISBN 9781433842894 (ebook)
Subjects: LCSH: Vocational guidance. | Career development. | BISAC: PSYCHOLOGY / Education & Training | PSYCHOLOGY / Industrial & Organizational Psychology
Classification: LCC HF5381 .T23578 2025 (print) | LCC HF5381 (ebook) | DDC 650.1--dc23/eng/20241209
LC record available at https://lccn.loc.gov/2024036351
LC ebook record available at https://lccn.loc.gov/2024036352

https://doi.org/10.1037/0000442-000

Printed in the United States of America

10 9 8 7 6 5 4 3 2 1

In heartfelt appreciation, this book is dedicated to Kathy and Craig Taylor, whose unwavering commitment to lifelong learning, curiosity, and endless support and love have indelibly shaped the tapestry of my being. Their influence, interwoven with the love and presence of my sister, Amanda Hilton; the steadfast support of my husband, Caner Derici; the companionship of little Dean, who was there with me during the final stages of this book; and the profound impact of my friends, colleagues, and extended family, has been a guiding thread in the fabric of who I am today. I would also like to extend a special acknowledgment to my grandparents, whose wisdom and life lessons have been the cornerstones in my journey.

In addition, the privilege of nurturing and guiding exceptionally talented students throughout my tenure as a professor has been a source of immeasurable honor. To the bright minds at the University of Florida, West Virginia University, Rowan University, and the University of Utah, as well as my cherished Lifelong Learning Lab family—Allie, Karen, Taylor, Erin, Mae, Ryan, Cat, and Carina—I dedicate this work with profound gratitude. Your collective thirst for knowledge and your dedication to the pursuit of wisdom and making this world a better, kinder place have enriched my life beyond measure.

—Jennifer M. Taylor

Contents

Series Preface   ix
Tony Rousmaniere and Alexandre Vaz

Acknowledgments   xiii

Part I   Overview and Instructions   1

CHAPTER 1. Introduction and Overview of Deliberate Practice and Career Counseling   3

CHAPTER 2. Instructions for the Career Counseling Deliberate Practice Exercises   17

Part II   Deliberate Practice Exercises for Career Counseling Skills   21

Exercises for Beginner Career Counseling Skills

EXERCISE 1. Exploring Your Client's Skills   23

EXERCISE 2. Exploring Your Client's Values   35

EXERCISE 3. Exploring Your Client's Decision-Making Styles   45

Exercises for Intermediate Career Counseling Skills

EXERCISE 4. Exploring Your Client's Cultural and Familial Influences   57

EXERCISE 5. Discussing the Benefits of Career Counseling   69

EXERCISE 6. Setting Session Goals   81

Exercises for Advanced Career Counseling Skills

EXERCISE 7. Feedback on Career Assessments   93

EXERCISE 8. Exploring Underlying Themes in Assessments   107

EXERCISE 9. Addressing Client Ambivalence and Skepticism   119

EXERCISE 10. Assigning Homework in Career Counseling   131

Comprehensive Exercises

EXERCISE 11. Annotated Career Counseling Practice Session Transcript   143

EXERCISE 12. Mock Career Counseling Sessions   151

Part III Strategies for Enhancing the Deliberate Practice Exercises   159

CHAPTER 3. How to Get the Most Out of Deliberate Practice: Additional Guidance for Trainers and Trainees   161

APPENDIX A. Difficulty Assessments and Adjustments   175
APPENDIX B. Deliberate Practice Diary Form   179
APPENDIX C. Sample Career Counseling Syllabus With Embedded Deliberate Practice Exercises   183

References   195
Index   203
About the Authors   207

Series Preface

Tony Rousmaniere and Alexandre Vaz

We are pleased to introduce the Essentials of Deliberate Practice series of training books. We are developing this book series to address a specific need that we see in many psychology training programs. The issue can be illustrated by the training experiences of Mary, a hypothetical second-year graduate school trainee. Mary has learned a lot about mental health theory, research, and counseling techniques. Mary is a dedicated student; she has read dozens of textbooks, written excellent papers about counseling, and receives near-perfect scores on her course exams. However, when Mary sits with her clients at her practicum site, she often has trouble performing the counseling skills that she can write and talk about so clearly. Furthermore, Mary has noticed herself getting anxious when her clients express strong reactions, such as getting very emotional, hopeless, or skeptical about counseling. Sometimes this anxiety is strong enough to make Mary freeze at key moments, limiting her ability to help those clients.

During her weekly individual and group supervision, Mary's supervisor gives her advice informed by empirically supported counseling techniques and common factor methods. The supervisor often supplements that advice by leading Mary through role-plays, recommending additional reading, or providing examples from her own work with clients. Mary, a dedicated supervisee who shares tapes of her sessions with her supervisor, is open about her challenges, carefully writes down her supervisor's advice, and reads the suggested readings. However, when Mary sits back down with her clients, she often finds that her new knowledge seems to have flown out of her head, and she is unable to enact her supervisor's advice. Mary finds this problem to be particularly acute with the clients who are emotionally evocative.

Mary's supervisor, who has received formal training in supervision, uses supervisory best practices, including the use of video to review supervisees' work. She would rate Mary's overall competence level as consistent with expectations for a trainee at Mary's developmental level. But even though Mary's overall progress is positive, she experiences some recurring problems in her work. This is true even though the supervisor is confident that she and Mary have identified the changes Mary should make in her work.

The problem with which Mary and her supervisor are wrestling—the disconnect between her knowledge about counseling and her ability to reliably perform counseling—is the focus of this book series. We started this series because most counselors experience this disconnect, to one degree or another, whether they are beginning trainees or highly experienced clinicians. In truth, we are all Mary.

To address this problem, we are focusing this series on the use of deliberate practice, a method of training specifically designed for improving reliable performance of complex skills in challenging work environments (Rousmaniere, 2016, 2019; Rousmaniere et al., 2017). Deliberate practice entails experiential, repeated training with a particular skill until it becomes automatic. In the context of counseling, this involves two trainees role-playing as a client and a counselor, switching roles every so often, under the guidance of a supervisor. The trainee playing the counselor reacts to client statements, ranging in difficulty from beginner to intermediate to advanced, with improvised responses that reflect fundamental counseling skills.

To create these books, we approached leading trainers and researchers of major therapy models with these simple instructions: Identify 10 to 12 essential skills for your therapy model where trainees often experience a disconnect between cognitive knowledge and performance ability—in other words, skills that trainees could write a good paper about but often have challenges performing, especially with challenging clients. We then collaborated with the authors to create deliberate practice exercises specifically designed to improve reliable performance of these skills and overall responsive treatment (Hatcher, 2015; Stiles et al., 1998; Stiles & Horvath, 2017). Finally, we rigorously tested these exercises with trainees and trainers at multiple sites around the world and refined them based on extensive feedback.

Each book in this series focuses on a specific therapy model, but readers will notice that most exercises in these books touch on common factor variables and facilitative interpersonal skills that researchers have identified as having the most impact on client outcome, such as empathy, verbal fluency, emotional expression, persuasiveness, and problem focus (e.g., Anderson et al., 2009; Norcross et al., 2019). Thus, the exercises in every book should help with a broad range of clients. Despite the specific theoretical model(s) from which counselors work, most counselors place a strong emphasis on pantheoretical elements of the therapeutic relationship, many of which have robust empirical support as correlates or mechanisms of client improvement (e.g., Norcross et al., 2019). We also recognize that therapy models have already-established training programs with rich histories, so we present deliberate practice not as a replacement but as an adaptable, transtheoretical training method that can be integrated into these existing programs to improve skill retention and help ensure basic competency.

About This Book

This book in the series focuses on career counseling skill development and is designed to help you feel more confident and supported when working with a range of career counseling clients. We encourage you to approach career counseling from a stance of curiosity and care. While this book delves into various career counseling techniques and skills, remember to draw upon your broader therapeutic skills as well, such as active listening, offering emphatic statements, and engaging with a genuine response.

In addition to encouraging your ongoing development of fundamental counseling skills, the exercises in this book will guide you in delving into your client's goals for career counseling, uncovering their innate skills, exploring their values, dissecting their decision-making styles, and examining the multifaceted impact of their cultural and familial backgrounds. Furthermore, you will find valuable guidance on seamlessly integrating career assessments into your counseling sessions, devising personalized homework assignments tailored to your client's unique needs, and skillfully addressing challenging issues such as client ambivalence and skepticism within the context of career counseling sessions.

Each exercise is designed to help you apply a diverse array of career counseling skills through focused practice sessions and ongoing feedback. This deliberate approach is intended to bolster your confidence and proficiency in working with clients who present a wide range of concerns. In this book, we adopt deliberate practice methods to support experiential—learn by doing—training opportunities. The described methods and stimuli can facilitate practicing a range of important career counseling skills. In addition, it supports fine-tuning the "how" of intervention delivery, including in a flexible manner across diverse career counseling scenarios. Importantly, this book is not intended to replace core coursework and exposure to foundational career counseling theories and principles of practice. Rather, this book is intended to augment other common training components.

Thank you for including us in your journey toward career counseling expertise. Now let's get to practice!

Acknowledgments

We would like to acknowledge Rodney Goodyear for his significant contribution to starting and organizing this book series. We are grateful to Susan Reynolds, David Becker, Elizabeth Budd, Joe Albrecht, and Emily Ekle at American Psychological Association (APA) Books for providing expert guidance and insightful editing that has significantly improved the quality and accessibility of this book. We would also like to acknowledge the International Deliberate Practice Society and its members for their many contributions and support for our work.

The exercises in this book series have undergone extensive testing at training programs around the world. More than 130 testers (trainees, therapists, and supervisors) from 16 countries contributed to testing the exercises. For everyone who volunteered to "test run" this work and provided critically important feedback throughout the method refinement and writing process, we cannot thank you enough.

I (Jennifer Taylor) would also like to express my heartfelt appreciation to my family, especially my mother, father, sister, grandparents, friends, and husband, for their unwavering support throughout this writing journey. In addition, I am immensely thankful for my mentors at the University of Florida, as well as my students and fellow faculty at West Virginia University and the University of Utah. I am also grateful to God for His ever-present love, goodness, and mercy throughout every stage of life. Lastly, I extend my profound gratitude to you, the reader, knowing that your commitment to knowledge and care for others will undoubtedly make a positive impact on countless career counseling clients you encounter.

Overview and Instructions

In Part I, we provide an overview of deliberate practice, including how it can be integrated into clinical training programs for career counseling, and instructions for performing the deliberate practice exercises in Part II. **We encourage both trainers and trainees to read both Chapters 1 and 2 before performing the deliberate practice exercises for the first time.**

Chapter 1 provides a foundation for the rest of the book by introducing important concepts related to deliberate practice and its role in psychotherapy training more broadly and career counseling training more specifically. We delve into the myriad ways in which career counseling can be harnessed to support clients with a diverse range of career counseling needs. We also offer a brief overview of 10 indispensable career counseling skills and integrate research on best practices in career counseling throughout the chapter.

Chapter 2 lays out the basic, most essential instructions for performing the career counseling deliberate practice exercises in Part II. They are designed to be quick and simple and provide you with just enough information to get started without being overwhelmed by too much information. Chapter 3 in Part III provides more in-depth guidance, which we encourage you to read once you are comfortable with the basic instructions in Chapter 2.

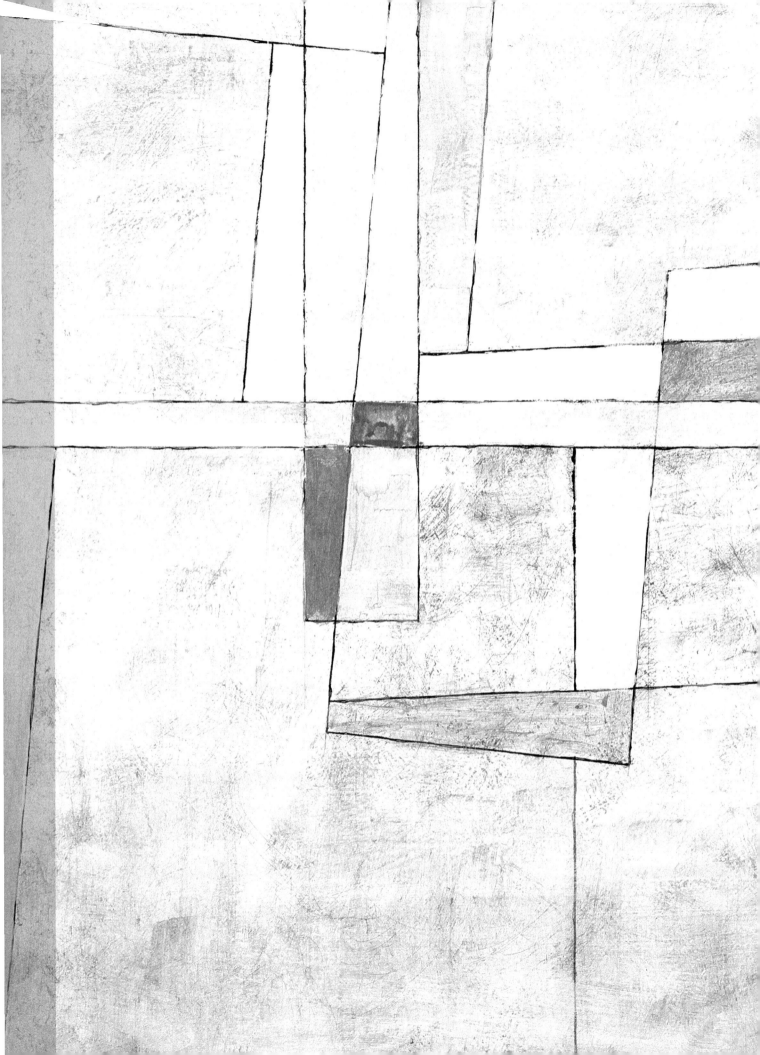

CHAPTER 1

Introduction and Overview of Deliberate Practice and Career Counseling

I (J. M. T.) remember my first day as a graduate student at a career counseling practicum site like it was yesterday. As I sat in my office, waiting with anticipation for my first client, I read through his intake form—a nontraditional, first-generation international college student with mounting bills, a tight graduate student stipend, a new baby, and little emotional and academic support from his graduate program and advisor. He was considering withdrawing from his graduate program but was very worried about disappointing his family—a family that had invested and sacrificed greatly for him to study in the United States. He didn't know what to do. And at the moment, neither did I. As I fumbled my way through our first session, I leaned on the general therapeutic skills I had learned through my counseling skills course—active listening, empathy, asking open-ended questions, unconditional positive regard, and instilling hope. They were great common factor skills, but they were skills that would only take me so far.

Our hope is that this book will serve as an invitation for you to build on the general counseling skills you've already been working to develop and to expand those skills to the world of career counseling. Many of the foundational skills you use every day when you work with clients (e.g., empathic listening, warmth, rapport building, cultural humility, promotion of hope) can be harnessed and seamlessly integrated with the 10 specific career counseling skills for which we will help you build self efficacy within this book. Whereas some books focus on theories, this book focuses on skill development and is designed to be a complement to a career counseling theories book and articles in the field of career counseling. We have intentionally focused this book with ongoing invitations to practice your developing career counseling skills because we know that some of the best ways to become a more confident and comfortable career counselor involve the process of hands-on learning, engaging in deliberate, ongoing practice, and receiving consistent, clear, and tailored feedback on your developing skills (see Jashinsky & King, 2019).

In their qualitative study of school counselors' experiences in career counseling and their self-assessments of their capabilities to provide career counseling to their students, Morgan et al. (2014) noted a common theme that spanned across all their

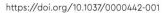

https://doi.org/10.1037/0000442-001

Deliberate Practice in Career Counseling, by J. M. Taylor, A. Vaz, and T. Rousmaniere

Copyright © 2025 by the American Psychological Association. All rights reserved.

participants: School counselors reported that they had learned many theories in their career counseling class, but felt a disconnect with their ability to apply relevant career counseling skills to their work with their students. And this lack of training and preparation created a gap that lowered their confidence in their career counseling abilities and impacted their ability to engage adequately with their students. Some of their participants even noted that they found themselves wishing their students wanted to talk about suicide or another subject matter in which they felt more competent rather than career counseling. The authors noted that all their participants experienced a sense of inadequacy and a lack of confidence in their capacity to provide effective career counseling to their students. They expressed frustration and attributed it to their perceived lack of skill-based training in their career counseling course. This issue is all the more concerning, as some participants also highlighted that, based on their experiences as school counselors now, career counseling was, perhaps, one of the most critical subject matter areas for school counselors in training.

This lack of confidence around career counseling may best be mitigated by learning specific skills, broken down into manageable pieces, practicing those skills again and again with mock clients in a low-risk environment, and receiving concrete and clear feedback along the way. We encourage you to approach the exercises in this book without expectations of perfection. Disregarding the fact that "perfection" is not a realistic expectation in any counseling sessions and the "perfect" session would look different with different clients and different counselors, if you already knew how to provide "perfect" career counseling session, there would be no purpose in taking a career counseling class, reading any career counseling books or articles, or practicing any skills. In fact, some of our very best learning comes from making mistakes. We expect that the first few times you try a new skill, you will fumble a bit—maybe even a lot. This is normal, and it's actually a good sign; it means that you're challenging yourself and you're growing. In fact, it's not just okay to make mistakes; it's actually good to make mistakes (Metcalfe, 2017)! When you make a mistake, we encourage you to treat it as you would a new painting you just created: Appreciate what you did well, look for areas of improvement and acknowledge any mishaps, sign your canvas by taking ownership of your work, and then? Begin again. Over time, with practice, support, and quality feedback, you will naturally grow in confidence and ease in these skills. Now that we've shared a brief rationale for deliberate practice as a meaningful way to enhance your career counseling skills, let's spend a moment introducing you to the career counseling deliberate practice exercises you will practice in this book.

Overview of the Deliberate Practice Exercises

The main focus of the book is a series of 12 exercises that have been thoroughly tested and modified based on feedback from trainers and trainees. The first 10 exercises each represent an essential career counseling skill. The last two exercises are more comprehensive, consisting of an annotated career counseling transcript and improvised mock counseling sessions that teach practitioners how to integrate all these skills into more expansive clinical scenarios. Table 1.1 presents the 10 skills that are covered in these exercises.

Throughout the exercises, trainees work in pairs under the guidance of a supervisor and role-play as a client and a career counselor, switching back and forth between the two roles. Each of the 10 skill-focused exercises consists of multiple client statements

TABLE 1.1. The 10 Career Counseling Skills Presented in the Deliberate Practice Exercises

Beginner Skills	Intermediate Skills	Advanced Skills
1. Exploring your client's skills 2. Exploring your client's values 3. Exploring your client's decision-making styles	4. Exploring your client's cultural and familial influences 5. Discussing the benefits of career counseling 6. Setting session goals	7. Feedback on career assessments 8. Exploring underlying themes in assessments 9. Addressing client ambivalence and skepticism 10. Assigning homework in career counseling

grouped by difficulty—beginner, intermediate, and advanced—that calls for a specific skill. For each skill, trainees are asked to read through and absorb the description of the skill, its criteria, and some examples of it. The trainee playing the client then reads the statements, which include presenting challenges, the client's goal for career counseling, their attitude toward career counseling, and their strengths. The trainee playing the career counselor then responds in a way that demonstrates the appropriate skill. Trainee career counselors will have the option of practicing a response using the one supplied in the exercise or immediately improvising and supplying their own.

After each client statement and career counselor response is practiced several times, the trainees will stop to receive feedback from the supervisor. Guided by the supervisor, the trainees will be instructed to try statement–responses several times, working their way down the list. In consultation with the supervisor, trainees will go through the exercises, starting with the least challenging and moving through to more advanced levels. The triad (supervisor–client–career counselor) will have the opportunity to discuss whether exercises present too much or too little challenge and adjust up or down depending on the assessment.

Trainees, in consultation with supervisors, can decide which skills they wish to work on and for how long. Based on our testing experience, we have found practice sessions last about 1 to 1.25 hours to receive maximum benefit. After this, trainees become saturated and need a break.

Ideally, career counselor learners will both gain confidence and achieve competence by practicing these exercises. Competence is defined here as the ability to perform a career counseling skill in a manner that is flexible and responsive to the client. Skills have been chosen that are considered essential to career counseling and that practitioners often find challenging to implement.

The skills identified in this book are not comprehensive in the sense of representing all one needs to learn to become a competent career counselor. Some will present particular challenges for trainees. A short history of career counseling and a brief description of the deliberate practice methodology is provided to explain how we have arrived at the union between them.

The Goals of This Book

The primary goal of this book is to help trainees achieve competence in core career counseling skills. Therefore, the expression of that skill or competency may look somewhat different across clients or even within a session with the same client.

The career counseling deliberate practice exercises are designed to achieve the following:

1. Help career counselors develop the ability to apply the skills in a range of counseling situations.

2. Move the skills into procedural memory (Squire, 2004) so that career counselors can access them even when they are tired, stressed, overwhelmed, or discouraged.

3. Provide career counselors in training with an opportunity to exercise the particular skill using a style and language that is congruent with who they are.

4. Provide the opportunity to use the career counseling skills in response to varying client statements and affects. This is designed to build confidence to adopt skills in a broad range of circumstances within different client contexts.

5. Provide career counselors in training with many opportunities to fail and then correct their failed response based on feedback. This helps build confidence and persistence.

Finally, this book aims to help trainees discover their own personal learning style so they can continue their professional development long after their formal training is concluded.

Who Can Benefit From This Book?

This book is designed to be used in multiple contexts, including in graduate-level courses, supervision, postgraduate training, and continuing education programs. It assumes the following:

1. The trainer is knowledgeable about and competent in career counseling.

2. The trainer is able to provide good demonstrations of how to use career counseling skills across a range of counseling situations, via role-play and/or video. Alternatively, the trainer has access to examples of career counseling being demonstrated through counseling videos.

3. The trainer is able to provide feedback to students regarding how to craft or improve their application of career counseling skills.

4. Trainees will have accompanying reading, such as books and articles, that explain the theory, research, and rationale for career counseling and each particular skill. Recommended reading for each skill is provided in the sample syllabus (Appendix C).

The exercises covered in this book series were piloted in training sites from 16 countries across four continents (North America, South America, Europe, and Asia). This book is designed for trainers and trainees from different cultural backgrounds worldwide.

This book is also designed for those who are training at all career stages, from beginning trainees, including those who have never worked with real clients, to seasoned career counselors. All exercises feature guidance for assessing and adjusting the difficulty to target the needs of each individual learner precisely. The term *trainee* in this book is used broadly, referring to anyone in the field of professional mental health who is endeavoring to acquire career counseling skills. For further guidance on how to improve multicultural deliberate practice skills, see the book *Deliberate Practice in Multicultural Therapy* (Harris et al., 2024).

Deliberate Practice in Counseling Training

How does one become an expert in their professional field? What is trainable and what is simply beyond our reach, due to innate or uncontrollable factors? Questions such as these touch on our fascination with expert performers and their development. A mixture of awe, admiration and even confusion surround people such as Mozart, da Vinci, or more contemporary top performers such as athletes Serena Williams, Michael Jordan, or Caitlin Clark and chess virtuoso Garry Kasparov. What accounts for their consistently superior professional results? Evidence suggests that the amount of or time spent on a particular type of training is a key factor in developing expertise in virtually all domains (Ericsson & Pool, 2016). Deliberate practice is an evidence-based method that can improve performance in an effective and reliable manner.

The concept of deliberate practice has its origins in a classic study by K. Anders Ericsson and colleagues (1993). They found that the amount of time practicing a skill and the quality of the time spent doing so were key factors predicting mastery and acquisition. They identified five key activities in learning and mastering skills: (a) observing one's own work, (b) getting expert feedback, (c) setting small incremental learning goals just beyond the performer's ability, (d) engaging in repetitive behavioral rehearsal of specific skills, and (e) continuously assessing performance. Ericsson and his colleagues termed this process deliberate practice, a cyclical process that is illustrated in Figure 1.1.

Research has shown that lengthy engagement in deliberate practice is associated with expert performance across a variety of professional fields, such as medicine, sports, music, chess, computer programming, and mathematics (Ericsson et al., 2018). People may associate deliberate practice with the widely known "10,000-hour rule" popularized by Malcolm Gladwell in his 2008 book *Outliers*, although the actual number of hours required for expertise varies by field and by individual (Ericsson & Pool, 2016). This, however, perpetuated two misunderstandings. First, that this is the number of

FIGURE 1.1. Cycle of Deliberate Practice

Note. From *Deliberate Practice in Emotion-Focused Therapy* (p. 7), by R. N. Goldman, A. Vaz, and T. Rousmaniere, 2021, American Psychological Association (https://doi.org/10.1037/0000227-000). Copyright 2021 by the American Psychological Association.

deliberate practice hours that everyone needs to attain expertise, no matter the domain. In fact, there can be considerable variability in how many hours are required.

The second misunderstanding is that engagement in 10,000 hours of work performance will lead one to become an expert in that domain. This misunderstanding holds considerable significance for the field of counseling and psychotherapy, where hours of work experience with clients has traditionally been used as a measure of proficiency (Rousmaniere, 2016). Research suggests that the amount of experience alone does not predict practitioner effectiveness (Goldberg, Rousmaniere, et al., 2016). It may be that the quality of deliberate practice is a key factor.

Practitioner scholars, recognizing the value of deliberate practice in other fields, have called for deliberate practice to be incorporated into training for mental health professionals (e.g., Bailey & Ogles, 2019; Hill et al., 2020; Rousmaniere et al., 2017; Taylor & Neimeyer, 2017; Tracey et al., 2015). There are, however, good reasons to question analogies made between career counseling and other professional fields, such as sports or music because by comparison, career counseling is so complex and free form. Sports have clearly defined goals, and classical music follows a written score. In contrast, the goals of career counseling shift with the unique presentation of each client at each session. Counselors do not have the luxury of following a score.

Instead, good counseling is more like improvisational jazz (Noa Kageyama, cited in Rousmaniere, 2016). In jazz improvisations, a complex mixture of group collaboration, creativity, and interaction are coconstructed among band members. Like career counseling, no two jazz improvisations are identical. However, improvisations are not a random collection of notes. They are grounded in a comprehensive theoretical understanding and technical proficiency that is only developed through continuous deliberate practice. For example, prominent jazz instructor Jerry Coker (1990) listed 18 skill areas that students must master, each of which has multiple discrete skills including tone quality, intervals, chord arpeggios, scales, patterns, and licks. In this sense, more creative and artful improvisations are actually a reflection of a previous commitment to repetitive skill practice and acquisition. As legendary jazz musician Miles Davis put it, "You have to play a long time to be able to play like yourself" (Cook, 2005, p. 112).

The main idea that we would like to stress here is that we want deliberate practice to help career counselors become themselves. The idea is to learn the skills so that you have them on hand when you want them. Practice the skills to make them your own. Incorporate those aspects that feel right for you. Ongoing and effortful deliberate practice should not be an impediment to flexibility and creativity. Ideally, it should enhance it. We recognize and celebrate that career counseling is an ever-shifting encounter and by no means want it to become or feel formulaic. Strong career counselors mix an eloquent integration of previously acquired skills with properly attuned flexibility. The core career counseling responses provided are meant as templates or possibilities, rather than "answers." Please interpret and apply them as you see fit, in a way that makes sense to you. We encourage flexible and improvisational play!

Simulation-Based Mastery Learning

Deliberate practice uses simulation-based mastery learning (Ericsson, 2004; McGaghie et al., 2014). That is, the stimulus material for training consists of "contrived social situations that mimic problems, events, or conditions that arise in professional encounters" (McGaghie et al., 2014, p. 375). A key component of this approach is that the stimuli being used in training are sufficiently similar to the real-world experiences so that they provoke similar reactions. This facilitates *state-dependent learning* in which professionals acquire skills in the same psychological environment where they will have to perform the skills (Fisher & Craik, 1977). For example, pilots train with flight simulators that present mechanical failures and dangerous weather conditions, and surgeons practice with surgical simulators that present medical complications. Training in simulations with challenging stimuli increases professionals' capacity to perform effectively under stress. For the career counseling training exercises in this book, the "simulators" are typical client statements that might actually be presented in the course of counseling sessions and call on the use of the particular skill.

Declarative Versus Procedural Knowledge

Declarative knowledge is what a person can understand, write, or speak about. It often refers to factual information that can be consciously recalled through memory and often acquired relatively quickly. In contrast, procedural learning is implicit in memory and "usually requires *repetition of an activity*, and associated learning is demonstrated through *improved task performance*" (Koziol & Budding, 2012, p. 2694, emphasis added). Procedural knowledge is what a person can perform, especially under stress (Squire, 2004). There can be a wide difference between their declarative and procedural knowledge. For example, an "armchair quarterback" is a person who understands and talks about athletics well but would have trouble performing it at a professional ability. Likewise, most dance, music, or theater critics have a high ability to write about their subjects but would be flummoxed if asked to perform them.

The sweet spot for deliberate practice is the gap between declarative and procedural knowledge. In other words, effortful practice should target those skills that the trainee could write a good paper about but would have trouble actually performing with a real client. We start with declarative knowledge, learning skills theoretically and observing others perform them. Once learned, with the help of deliberate practice, we work toward the development of procedural learning, with the aim of counselors having "automatic" access to each of the skills that they can call on when necessary.

Let us turn to a brief theoretical background on career counseling to help contextualize the skills of the book and how they fit into the greater training model.

Overview of Career Counseling

"So . . . what do you do?" In some cultures, this is often one of the first questions asked when meeting someone new—as common, perhaps, as asking how someone is doing or what their name is. But underneath that question lies an important reality; for many, their identities—even their worth—are linked with their job titles. They define who they are by what they do.

This enmeshment—or lack thereof—between a person's job title and their personal identity can create significant identity dissonance. When people do not feel that the two are aligned, when they lose their jobs, when they fail at work, or when they don't get that promotion they've been working so hard for, those experiences can create conflicts that commonly bring clients into our offices.

However, enmeshment is just one of many reasons people may find themselves in need of career support and a metaphorical lifeline. In some cultures, where "workaholism" is admired and respected, burnout and poor health become constant companions (Abramson, 2022; American Psychological Association, 2021; Andreassen, 2014) and can lead to significant distress if not addressed (Maslach & Leiter, 2016; Papathanasiou,

2015). In addition, research by other scholars suggests that the pressure to find one's "calling" can leave college students feeling uneasy, confused, and indecisive (Duffy & Sedlacek, 2007).

The issues people experience today are issues people experienced decades, even centuries ago as well. As one example, the economic depression of 1873 had an impact on many Americans, including Frank Parsons, who lost his job after his employer fell into bankruptcy. In 1908, Parsons, who is often referred to as the "father" of the vocational guidance movement, created the Vocation Bureau of Boston to assist others who were unemployed and were looking for a career. From his experiences and the vocational program he created arose the first principles of vocational choice; Ralph Elbertson identified five of Parsons's principles in Parsons's (1909) book, and Jones (1994) has since identified five additional principles from Parsons. Three key components of the first career development theory include the following: (a) a thorough self-understanding of one's skills, interests, goals, resources, and barriers and their causes; (b) an understanding of particular career paths (e.g., the needs of an employer and requirements for success, the advantages and disadvantages of specific careers, opportunities within other careers); and (c) what Parsons's termed "true reasoning," or decision making and career planning based on knowledge of oneself and knowledge of careers (Parsons, 1909, p. 5). Exploring these three areas set the foundation for numerous career theories that have since followed.

The good news that we know decades later is that career counseling works. Research suggests that career counseling can have both short-term and long-term positive effects for clients (Perdrix et al., 2012). One key ingredient of career counseling success may be the counselors themselves. Whiston (2020) summarized both historical and recent meta-analyses on the components of effective career counseling. Among the findings summarized by the author, many studies suggest that the support clients feel from their career counselors plays an integral role in the usefulness of career counseling (see also Whiston et al., 2017).

While we're talking about support, we would like to acknowledge that trainees often worry that they should be the expert and should have all the answers to solve their clients' problems. We want to gently remind you that it is not your responsibility to solve your client's problems but rather to collaborate with them to engage in meaningful reflection; to create an open space for clients to share their experiences, thoughts, and feelings; and to invite them on a journey together to explore future options. The exercises in this book are designed to help you do just that. We have gathered in this book skills that build on decades of research (see Soares et al., 2022) that highlight common career counseling tasks—tasks such as exploration of skills, values, and personal interests; job search training; career decision-making training; and more.

In addition to gaining comfort and familiarity with common career counseling tasks through the 10 exercises in this book, approaching career counseling with a multicultural orientation through cultural humility, cultural comfort, and cultural opportunities (Davis et al., 2018) is particularly crucial. We invite you to take one practical first step by committing some time to self-exploration. Consider your earliest career hopes and dreams; your past career experiences; biases and assumptions you hold about different careers; the ways in which mentors have shaped you thus far; the messages you've received from friends, family, and your salient cultures surrounding the topic of careers; careers you've felt were "off limits" for you and why; how society has shaped your career path and what careers were or felt attainable; and events that have shaped your educational and career decisions. The more you are aware of your own history, biases, assumptions, and experiences, the less your story will inadvertently bleed into your sessions with your clients.

Career Counseling Skills in Deliberate Practice

Now that we've discussed the relevance of careers in everyday life, provided a brief history of career counseling, and discussed the importance of multicultural orientation and self-reflection, let's situate career counseling skills in the context of deliberate practice itself. In this next section, we delve into the three categories of skills in this book and discuss each skill in more detail so that you will know what to expect from this book and how these exercises help you.

Categorizing Career Counseling Skills

The 10 career counseling skills in this book are categorized in two ways. The first way they are categorized is by their perceived difficulty level. Three of the skills are categorized as "beginner" skills, three additional skills are categorized as "intermediate," and four of the skills are categorized as "advanced."

The second way the skills are categorized is by their relevant themes. The first three beginning skills focus on fostering personal insight and self-exploration. These skills will enable you to better understand who your client is, what's important to them, and how they approach a range of situations and life decisions. The following four intermediate skills concentrate on guidance and goal setting. Within these four skills, you will learn how to explore the impact of your client's cultures and family on their education and career decisions, you will learn how to discuss with verbal fluency why career counseling could be useful for your client, and you will learn how to set personalized session goals with your client. Collaboratively crafting session goals will create greater focus and clarity for your career counseling sessions and will build a roadmap for your interventions and even future homework assignments for your client. The final three advanced skills focus on integrative skills. These will support you in tying career assessment results together, linking themes across assessment findings, listening to the client's underlying messages and addressing their concerns, and assigning homework tailored to each client's specific needs. As a career counselor, you may provide group counseling as well. Many of the skills you will learn can be adapted and used in group career counseling sessions as well.

Comprehensive Exercises

In addition to the 10 career counseling skills introduced in this book, we also share two comprehensive exercises for you. Exercise 11 provides you with an annotated career counseling practice session transcript. This exercise will allow you to visualize the 10 skills integrated and in action. Then, after practicing each of the skills through the 10 exercises provided and reviewing an annotated career counseling session transcript, you will have the opportunity to practice integrating the career counseling skills you have developed through improvisational role-plays of more extensive career counseling sessions. This final exercise, Exercise 12, will support you by increasing your confidence in incorporating the skills you have developed across this learning experience in comprehensive career counseling sessions. The more you practice, the more natural and fluid your sessions will become.

The Career Counseling Skills Presented in Exercises 1–10

Now that we've discussed a brief overview and rationale for the exercises, let's delve into a brief description of each skill.

Beginner Exercises

Exercise 1: Exploring Your Client's Skills. Through this exercise, you will boost your confidence in helping clients integrate their skills into their current or future career. You will also collaborate with your client to identify potential career paths that align with and capitalize on their skill sets.

Exercise 2: Exploring Your Client's Values. In addition to exploring skills, you will also learn how to help your client explore their values. In this exercise, you will assist them in examining ways they could integrate those values more intentionally in their current job or use those values to inform future vocational or avocational decisions (e.g., using values to narrow down potential career paths or to inform questions a client could ask during job interviews, exploring hobbies that could help your client align their values in life outside of work).

Exercise 3: Exploring Your Client's Decision-Making Styles. The topic of decision making has gained significant research attention as an important construct in career counseling (Soares et al., 2022). By completing Exercise 3, you will learn how to help clients who are stumped and stalled by indecision. Rather than beginning by suggesting solutions to their indecision, you will explore what they have tried thus far to attempt to address their uncertainty. You will then work with your client to brainstorm a task to address their indecision.

Intermediate Exercises

Exercise 4: Exploring Your Client's Cultural and Familial Influences. Exercise 4 invites you and your client to delve into the cultural and familial messages that have shaped your client's view of particular careers, your client's salient collective values, and the messages they have received through observing the career experiences of family members and others in their cultural community.

Exercise 5: Discussing the Benefits of Career Counseling. This exercise will help you become more comfortable discussing the ways in which career counseling could be beneficial for your client. The purpose and personal benefits of career counseling will necessarily differ, depending on each client's individual needs and presenting concerns. This skill is particularly helpful to address client ambivalence or skepticism, which we discuss in more detail in Exercise 9.

Exercise 6: Setting Session Goals. Utilizing this skill, you will be able to work collaboratively to create session goals that are tailored to your client's presenting concerns. This skill will help you build focus and direction in your sessions and will support you and your client in monitoring progress in career counseling.

Advanced Exercises

Exercise 7: Feedback on Career Assessments. After gaining confidence in exploring your client's skills, values, decision-making styles, and cultural and familial influences, you'll be ready to head into some of the more advanced career counseling skills. Exercise 7 focuses on providing feedback to your clients on their career assessment results. You will learn how to highlight a primary observation from your client's assessment results, you will note important caveats about the limitations of assessment results that help contextualize any assessment report recommendations, and you will learn how to create space for your client to share their thoughts and reactions to their assessment results.

Exercise 8: Exploring Underlying Themes in Assessments. Exercise 8 builds on the foundational skills developed in Exercise 7. In Exercise 8, you will gain competence in uncovering underlying themes across your client's assessment results and will practice inviting your client to reflect on the underlying theme you pose.

Exercise 9: Addressing Client Ambivalence and Skepticism. In this exercise, you'll master the art of navigating some particularly challenging situations counselors face: client ambivalence and skepticism. This skill will empower you to engage with your clients effectively, bridging the gap in counseling and meeting them where they are. Rather than dismissing their feelings or attempting to persuade them otherwise, you'll learn techniques to ask open-ended questions that encourage clients to identify reasons career counseling could be beneficial.

Exercise 10: Assigning Homework in Career Counseling. This final skill will equip you to offer clients meaningful homework assignments that address their current concerns and align with their career counseling goals. We will introduce you to a variety of potential assignments for clients who wish to work on their career concerns beyond your counseling sessions. Through this exercise, you will become adept at creatively engaging your clients outside of the career counseling sessions. This will enable clients to maximize their career counseling experience and will motivate them to actively explore and shape their career decisions.

A Note About Vocal Tone, Facial Expression, and Body Posture

Although we have briefly introduced you to the 10 career counseling skills in this book, we would be remiss if we didn't also touch briefly on the importance of our nonverbal communication and our tone as career counselors. Nonverbal communication plays a critical role in the counseling session and in one's ability to express themselves (Mitzkovitz et al., 2022). Counselors can improve their multicultural competence by paying attention to the nonverbal communication in a counseling session (Mariska & Harrawood, 2013).

So what does appropriate nonverbal communication look like in career counseling? We want to note at the outset that attending to microexpressions and nonverbal communication are equally as important in career counseling as they are in personal counseling. When providing career counseling, we encourage you to approach your clients with warmth, humility, empathy, open-mindedness, and curiosity. An open posture, expressing positive regard, appropriate eye contact (which, importantly, can vary from culture to culture; see Uono & Hietanen, 2015), nonverbal cues (e.g., nodding; displaying a responsive emotion facially, such as smiling or frowning), mirroring, and respecting your client's personal space, recognizing this may differ across cultures, are all important nonverbal skills to attend to in your sessions.

The Role of Deliberate Practice in Career Counseling Training

As noted earlier, research suggests that counselors frequently report feeling ill-equipped to provide career counseling, largely because career counseling classes often focus on career development theories but lack a focus on helping students build tangible career counseling skills (Morgan et al., 2014). Deliberate practice offers a practical anecdote to address this common issue. The more you hone these skills through practice, the more at ease you will feel during your client sessions.

Overview of the Book's Structure

This book is organized into three parts. Part I contains this chapter and Chapter 2, which provides basic instructions on how to perform these exercises. We found through testing that providing too many instructions upfront overwhelmed trainers and trainees, and as a result, they skipped past them. Therefore, we kept these instructions as brief and simple as possible to focus only on the most essential information that trainers and trainees will need to get started with the exercises. Further guidelines for getting the most out of deliberate practice are provided in Chapter 3, and additional instructions for monitoring and adjusting the difficulty of the exercises are provided in Appendix A. **Do not skip the instructions in Chapter 2, and be sure to read the additional guidelines and instructions in Chapter 3 and Appendix A once you are comfortable with the basic instructions.**

Part II contains the 10 skill-focused exercises, which are ordered based on their difficulty: beginner, intermediate, and advanced (see Table 1.1). They each contain a brief overview of the exercise, example client–career counselor interactions to help guide trainees, a list of criteria for mastering the relevant skill, and step-by-step instructions for conducting that exercise. The client statements and sample career counselor responses are then presented, also organized by difficulty (beginner, intermediate, and advanced). The statements and responses are presented separately so that the trainee playing the career counselor has more freedom to improvise responses without being influenced by the sample responses, which should only be turned to if the trainee has difficulty improvising their own. The last two exercises in Part II provide opportunities to practice the 10 skills within simulated career counseling sessions. Exercise 11 provides a sample career counseling session transcript in which the career counseling skills are used and clearly labeled, thereby demonstrating how they might flow together in an actual career counseling session. Career counseling trainees are invited to run through the sample transcript with one playing the career counselor and the other playing the client to get a feel for how a session might unfold. Exercise 12 provides suggestions for undertaking mock sessions, as well as client profiles ordered by difficulty (beginner, intermediate, and advanced) that trainees can use for improvised role-plays.

Part III contains Chapter 3, which provides additional guidance for trainers and trainees. While Chapter 2 is more procedural, Chapter 3 covers big-picture issues. It highlights six key points for getting the most out of deliberate practice and describes the importance of appropriate responsiveness, attending to trainee well-being and respecting their privacy, and trainer self-evaluation, among other topics.

Three appendixes conclude this book. Appendix A provides instructions for monitoring and adjusting the difficulty of each exercise as needed. It provides a Deliberate Practice Reaction Form for the trainee playing the career counselor to complete to indicate whether the exercise is too easy or too difficult. Appendix B includes a Deliberate Practice Diary Form that can be used during a training session's final evaluation to process the trainees' experiences, but its primary purpose is to provide trainees a format to explore and record their experiences while engaging in additional, between-session deliberate practice activities without the supervisor. Appendix C presents a sample syllabus demonstrating how the 10 deliberate practice exercises and other support material can be integrated into a wider career counseling training course. Instructors may choose to modify the syllabus or pick elements of it to integrate into their own courses.

Downloadable versions of this book's appendixes, including a color version of the Deliberate Practice Reaction Form, can be found in the "Resources" tab online (https://www.apa.org/pubs/books/deliberate-practice-career-counseling).

Instructions for the Career Counseling Deliberate Practice Exercises

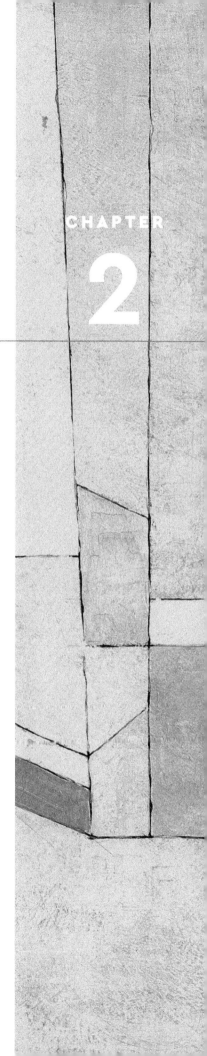

CHAPTER 2

This chapter provides basic instructions that are common to all the exercises in this book. More specific instructions are provided in each exercise. Chapter 3 also provides important guidance for trainees and trainers that will help them get the most out of deliberate practice. Appendix A offers additional instructions for monitoring and adjusting the difficulty of the exercises as needed after getting through all the client statements in a single difficulty level, including a Deliberate Practice Reaction Form the trainee playing the career counselor can complete to indicate whether they found the statements too easy or too difficult. **Difficulty assessment is an important part of the deliberate practice process and should not be skipped.**

Overview

The deliberate practice exercises in this book involve role-plays of hypothetical situations in career counseling. The role-plays involve three people: One trainee role-plays the career counselor, another trainee role-plays the client, and a trainer (professor/supervisor) observes and provides feedback. Alternatively, a peer can observe and provide feedback.

This book provides a script for the role-plays, each with a client statement and also with an example career counselor response. The client statements are graded in difficulty from beginner to advanced, although these difficulty grades are only estimates. The actual perceived difficulty of client statements is subjective and varies widely by trainee. For example, some trainees may experience a stimulus of a client being angry to be easy to respond to, whereas another trainee may experience it as very difficult. Thus, it is important for trainees to provide difficulty assessments and adjustments to ensure that they are practicing at the right difficulty level: neither too easy nor too hard.

---

https://doi.org/10.1037/0000442-002
Deliberate Practice in Career Counseling, by J. M. Taylor, A. Vaz, and T. Rousmaniere
Copyright © 2025 by the American Psychological Association. All rights reserved.

Time Frame

We recommend a 90-minute time block for every exercise, structured roughly as follows:

- First 20 minutes: Orientation. The trainer explains the career counseling skill and demonstrates the exercise procedure with a volunteer trainee.
- Middle 50 minutes: Trainees perform the exercise in pairs. The trainer or a peer provides feedback throughout this process and monitors/adjusts the exercise's difficulty as needed after each set of statements (see Appendix A for more information about difficulty assessment).
- Final 20 minutes: Review, feedback, and discussion.

Preparation

1. Every trainee will need their own copy of this book.
2. Each exercise requires the trainer to fill out a Deliberate Practice Reaction Form after completing all the statements from a single difficulty level. This form is available in the "Resources" tab online (https://www.apa.org/pubs/books/deliberate-practice-career-counseling) and in Appendix A.
3. Trainees are grouped into pairs. One volunteers to role-play the career counselor and one to role-play the client (they will switch roles after 15 minutes of practice). As noted previously, an observer who might be either the trainer or a fellow trainee will work with each pair.

The Role of the Trainer

The primary responsibilities of the trainer are as follows:

1. Provide corrective feedback, which includes both information about how well the trainees' response met expected criteria and any necessary guidance about how to improve the response.
2. Remind trainees to do difficulty assessments and adjustments after each level of client statements is completed (beginner, intermediate, and advanced).

How to Practice

Each exercise includes its own step-by-step instructions. Trainees should follow these instructions carefully, as every step is important.

Skill Criteria

Each of the first 10 exercises focuses on one essential career counseling skill with two to three skill criteria that describe the important components or principles for that skill.

The goal of the role-play is for trainees to practice improvising responses to the client statement in a manner that (a) is attuned to the client, (b) meets skill criteria

as much as possible, and (c) feels authentic for the trainee. Trainees are provided scripts with example career counselor responses to give them a sense of how to incorporate the skill criteria into a response. **It is important, however, that trainees do not read the example responses verbatim in the role-plays!** Career counseling is highly personal and improvisational; the goal of deliberate practice is to develop trainees' ability to improvise within a consistent framework. Memorizing scripted responses would be counterproductive for helping trainees learn to perform career counseling that is responsive, authentic, and attuned to each individual client.

Drs. Taylor and Vaz wrote the scripted example responses, but trainees' personal style of career counseling may differ slightly or greatly from that in the example scripts. It is essential that, over time, trainees develop their own style and voice, while simultaneously being able to intervene according to the model's principles and strategies. To facilitate this, the exercises in this book were designed to maximize opportunities for improvisational responses informed by the skill criteria and ongoing feedback.

Review, Feedback, and Discussion

The review and feedback sequence after each role-play has these two elements:

- First, the trainee who played the client **briefly** shares how it felt to be on the receiving end of the career counselor's response. This can help assess how well trainees are attuning with the client.

- Second, the trainer provides **brief** feedback (less than 1 minute) based on the skill criteria for each exercise. Keep feedback specific, behavioral, and brief to preserve time for skill rehearsal. If one trainer is teaching multiple pairs of trainees, the trainer walks around the room, observing the pairs and offering brief feedback. When the trainer is not available, the trainee playing the client gives peer feedback to the career counselor, based on the skill criteria and how it felt to be on the receiving end of the intervention. Alternatively, a third trainee can observe and provide feedback.

Trainers (or peers) should remember to keep all feedback specific and brief and not to veer into discussions of theory. There are many other settings for extended discussion of career counseling theory and research. In deliberate practice, it is of utmost importance to maximize time for continuous behavioral rehearsal via role-plays.

Final Evaluation

After both trainees have role-played the client and the career counselor, the trainer provides an evaluation. Participants should engage in a short group discussion based on this evaluation. This discussion can provide ideas for where to focus homework and future deliberate practice sessions. To this end, Appendix B presents a Deliberate Practice Diary Form, which can also be downloaded from the "Resources" tab online (https://www.apa.org/pubs/books/deliberate-practice-career-counseling). This form can be used by trainees as part of the final feedback to help them process their experiences from that session with the supervisor. However, it is designed primarily to be used as a template for exploring and recording their thoughts and experiences between sessions, particularly when pursuing additional deliberate practice activities without the supervisor, such as rehearsing responses alone or if two trainees want practice the exercises together, perhaps with a third trainee filling the supervisor's role. Then, if they want, the trainees can discuss these experiences with the supervisor at the beginning of the next training session.

Deliberate Practice Exercises for Career Counseling Skills

This section of the book provides 10 deliberate practice exercises for essential career counseling skills. These exercises are organized in a developmental sequence, from those that are more appropriate for someone just beginning career counseling training to those who have progressed to a more advanced level. Although we anticipate that most trainers will use these exercises in the order we have suggested, some trainers may find it more appropriate to their training circumstances to use a different order than presented in the thematic ordering section noted in Chapter 1. We also provide two comprehensive exercises that bring together the career counseling skills using an annotated career counseling session transcript and mock career counseling sessions.

Exercises for Beginner Career Counseling Skills
EXERCISE 1: Exploring Your Client's Skills   23
EXERCISE 2: Exploring Your Client's Values   35
EXERCISE 3: Exploring Your Client's Decision-Making Styles   45

Exercises for Intermediate Career Counseling Skills
EXERCISE 4: Exploring Your Client's Cultural and Familial Influences   57
EXERCISE 5: Discussing the Benefits of Career Counseling   69
EXERCISE 6: Setting Session Goals   81

Exercises for Advanced Career Counseling Skills
EXERCISE 7: Feedback on Career Assessments   93
EXERCISE 8: Exploring Underlying Themes in Assessments   107
EXERCISE 9: Addressing Client Ambivalence and Skepticism   119
EXERCISE 10: Assigning Homework in Career Counseling   131

Comprehensive Exercises
EXERCISE 11: Annotated Career Counseling Practice Session Transcript   143
EXERCISE 12: Mock Career Counseling Sessions   151

Exercise 1

Exploring Your Client's Skills

Preparations for Exercise 1

1. Read the instructions in Chapter 2.
2. Download the Deliberate Practice Reaction Form and the Deliberate Practice Diary Form at https://www.apa.org/pubs/books/deliberate-practice-career-counseling (see the "Resources" tab; also available in Appendixes A and B, respectively).

Skill Description

Skill Difficulty Level: Beginner

Inviting your clients to explore their strengths can help them consider how they can harness them more effectively in their current career or consider alternative careers that might capitalize on those strengths. This is a great skill to use with clients who are unhappy, uninspired, or unmotivated in their current career.

Please note that although this is an essential skill, clients sometimes struggle to name their strengths. There may be several reasons why your client may not discuss their skills or strengths or may be unable to do so. For example, in some cultures, it may be viewed as inappropriate or boastful to discuss personal strengths (Clark & Molinsky, 2014). Others may be plagued by feelings of imposterism, a finding common across cultures and professions (Bravata et al., 2020; Clark et al., 2014; Dana Ménard & Chittle, 2023; Sawant et al., 2023). Furthermore, when you find yourself guessing or making assumptions about the skills you believe your client possesses based on what they have shared, remember to consult with them to confirm whether the skills or strengths you are emphasizing align with their perspectives and feel authentic to them. For more resources, refer back to Chapter 1 of this book.

https://doi.org/10.1037/0000442-003

Deliberate Practice in Career Counseling, by J. M. Taylor, A. Vaz, and T. Rousmaniere

Copyright © 2025 by the American Psychological Association. All rights reserved.

In this exercise, the counselor should improvise a response to each client statement following these skill criteria:

1. **Paraphrase the skill reflected by the client.** The first skill criterion requires careful active listening on your part. Your client may not always explicitly name a strength. For example, if your client states that they were a leader in their impromptu speech and debate team, ask yourself what underlying skills are involved in that role and highlight them.

2. **After paraphrasing the skill reflected by the client, the counselor does one of the following:**
   - **Option A: Ask the client how they could use that skill more in their current or future job.** This skill is appropriate for clients who are already employed but perhaps dissatisfied with their current job or looking to expand their current job. Your task here is to invite your client to consider ways that they could more intentionally embed their named skills in their current career.
   - **Option B: Ask the client to reflect on potential jobs that would capitalize on that skill set.** This skill is designed for clients who are in a career exploration stage. In this option, you will encourage your client to consider career paths that might capitalize and value their specific skill set.

Note. Feel free to choose either option to fulfill Criterion 2, but we encourage you to alternate your response options so that you do not over-rely on one technique to the detriment of the other.

SKILL CRITERIA FOR EXERCISE 1

1. Paraphrase the skill reflected by the client.
2. After paraphrasing the skill, the counselor does one of the following:
   - Option A: Ask the client how they could use that skill more in their current or future job.
   - Option B: Ask the client to reflect on potential jobs that would capitalize on that skill set.

Examples of Counselors Exploring Their Client's Skills

Example 1

CLIENT: [*proud*] Mom always told me I'm a good listener.

COUNSELOR: It sounds like you're able to really hold space for others. (Criterion 1) In what ways do you spend time listening to others in your current job? How could you do that more intentionally? (Criterion 2, Option A)

or

In thinking about the careers you're considering, what careers would allow you time and space to listen to others? (Criterion 2, Option B)

Example 2

CLIENT: [*happy*] I'm really good at working with coworkers on projects. Having multiple perspectives really makes our work stronger.

COUNSELOR: That's a great strength! Having a skill in the area of teamwork is very valuable for many employers. (Criterion 1) Do you work in teams in your current job? In what ways could you do more of that? (Criterion 2, Option A)

or

I wonder what careers would provide you with opportunities to work with others? (Criterion 2, Option B)

Example 3

CLIENT: [*confident*] Last year I won the Graduate Student Teacher of the Year Award!

COUNSELOR: Wow, what an accomplishment! It sounds like your teaching skills are being well-recognized! (Criterion 1) In thinking about your current job responsibilities and everyday tasks, in what ways could you lean into your skills around teaching, instructing, or mentoring others more? (Criterion 2, Option A)

or

Given your strengths in teaching, I'd invite you to think for a moment about careers you're considering that might capitalize on that strength. (Criterion 2, Option B)

INSTRUCTIONS FOR EXERCISE 1
Step 1: Role-Play and Feedback
- The client says the first beginner client statement. The counselor **improvises** a response based on the skill criteria. - The trainer (or, if not available, the client) provides **brief** feedback based on the skill criteria. - The client then repeats the same statement, and the counselor again improvises a response. The trainer (or client) again provides brief feedback.
Step 2: Repeat
- Repeat Step 1 for all the statements **in the current difficulty level** (beginner, intermediate, or advanced).
Step 3: Assess and Adjust Difficulty
- The counselor completes the Deliberate Practice Reaction Form (see Appendix A) and decides whether to make the exercise easier or harder or to repeat the same difficulty level.
Step 4: Repeat for Approximately 15 Minutes
- Repeat Steps 1 to 3 for at least 15 minutes. - The trainees then switch counselor and client roles and start over.

Now it's your turn! Follow Steps 1 and 2 from the instructions.

Remember: The goal of the role-play is for trainees to practice improvising responses to the client statements in a manner that (a) uses the skill criteria and (b) feels authentic for the trainee. **Example counselor responses for each client statement are provided at the end of this exercise. Trainees should attempt to improvise their own responses before reading the examples.**

BEGINNER-LEVEL CLIENT STATEMENTS FOR EXERCISE 1
Beginner Client Statement 1
[Assertive] My family always told me I'm a natural-born leader.
Beginner Client Statement 2
[Interested] Hmmm . . . I've never really thought about my strengths before . . . but I guess I can see the bigger picture without overemphasizing the small details?
Beginner Client Statement 3
[Thoughtfully] My mom always told me I was good at art, music, and writing.
Beginner Client Statement 4
[Speaking quickly] People at work notice that I think quickly.
Beginner Client Statement 5
[Confidently] My friends tell me I'm really good at giving advice.

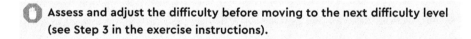 **Assess and adjust the difficulty before moving to the next difficulty level (see Step 3 in the exercise instructions).**

INTERMEDIATE-LEVEL CLIENT STATEMENTS FOR EXERCISE 1
Intermediate Client Statement 1
[Proudly] When I was in high school, my friends always asked me to proofread their papers . . . and they always got As from their teachers afterward!
Intermediate Client Statement 2
[Quietly] My friends always come to me when they have problems and tell me they feel so much lighter after they leave.
Intermediate Client Statement 3
[Self-assured] Writing always came natural for me. It's been a fun way to express myself!
Intermediate Client Statement 4
[Curious] I usually make decisions based on what "feels" right—what my gut tells me to do . . . and usually, it works out well!
Intermediate Client Statement 5
[Assertively] I was the top sales consultant for the last company I worked for—they even gave me a plaque!

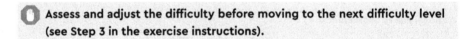 **Assess and adjust the difficulty before moving to the next difficulty level (see Step 3 in the exercise instructions).**

ADVANCED-LEVEL CLIENT STATEMENTS FOR EXERCISE 1
Advanced Client Statement 1
[Reflective] I guess I never really thought about my strengths. Um . . . I map out my tasks with my planner every day. Maybe I need to schedule some time to think about my strengths!
Advanced Client Statement 2
[Matter-of-factly] I'm really good at tinkering with things and fixing them. I once fixed a broken LCD screen on a TV.
Advanced Client Statement 3
[Respected] My boss gave me a salary bonus at my summer job at the computer repair store because I had the best record for quickly finding the causes of problems and deciding what to do about it.
Advanced Client Statement 4
[Shame] I don't think I have any skills. I just spend all day baking for myself.
Advanced Client Statement 5
[Boastful] I was the leader of my impromptu speech and debate team in high school!

> **Assess and adjust the difficulty here (see Step 3 in the exercise instructions). If appropriate, follow the instructions to make the exercise even more challenging (see Appendix A).**

Example Counselor Responses: Exploring Your Client's Skills

Remember: Trainees should attempt to improvise their own responses before reading the examples. **Do not read the following responses verbatim unless you are having trouble coming up with your own!**

EXAMPLE RESPONSES TO BEGINNER-LEVEL CLIENT STATEMENTS FOR EXERCISE 1
Example Response to Beginner Client Statement 1
Leadership is a fabulous strength! (Criterion 1) What leadership roles do you aspire to in your current job? In what ways could you engage in more leadership at work? (Criterion 2, Option A) or In thinking about some of your dream jobs, which ones involve leadership roles? (Criterion 2, Option B)
Example Response to Beginner Client Statement 2
That's a perspective skill that many wish for—the ability not to get so lost in the trees that we miss the forest! (Criterion 1) In what ways could you build more on your strength of being able to see the bigger picture in your current job? (Criterion 2, Option A) or As you think about careers you're considering, which ones would allow you to take a bird's-eye view on issues? Which ones would require that you focus more on specific details? (Criterion 2, Option B)
Example Response to Beginner Client Statement 3
Sounds like you have many creative talents! (Criterion 1) In what ways could you infuse creativity more in your current job? (Criterion 1, Option A) or As you think about the careers you're considering, which ones involve a creative component and how? (Criterion 2, Option B)
Example Response to Beginner Client Statement 4
I'm sure it's come in handy to have quick-thinking skills! (Criterion 1) How might you capitalize more on your ability to think on your feet at your current job? (Criterion 2, Option A) or Which professions do you think would most value your ability to think quickly? (Criterion 2, Option B)
Example Response to Beginner Client Statement 5
I'm sure they appreciate you listening to them and offering ideas to help. (Criterion 1) Given your strengths in listening and brainstorming good ideas, in what ways could you listen and support others more at work? (Criterion 2, Option A) or As you think about all the careers you've been considering, which ones would value your listening skills and ability to advise others? (Criterion 2, Option B)

EXAMPLE RESPONSES TO INTERMEDIATE-LEVEL CLIENT STATEMENTS FOR EXERCISE 1

Example Response to Intermediate Client Statement 1

You must have a good eye for detail! (Criterion 1) How might you continue to capitalize on your attention to detail in your current job? (Criterion 2, Option A)

or

Of the careers you're considering, which ones would require a good eye for detail? (Criterion 2, Option B)

Example Response to Intermediate Client Statement 2

It sounds like you're a great listener to them. Since they feel lighter when they leave, I imagine you're a great empathizer too! (Criterion 1) Give this strength of yours, as you think about your current job, how might you engage in more active listening with others? (Criterion 2, Option A)

or

What career paths value active listening and empathy? (Criterion 2, Option B)

Example Response to Intermediate Client Statement 3

You sound skilled in the creative process! (Criterion 1) In what ways might you infuse more creativity in your current job? (Criterion 1, Option A)

or

In thinking about the careers you are considering, which ones would provide you the most opportunities to be creative and to express your ideas? (Criterion 2, Option B)

Example Response to Intermediate Client Statement 4

Yeah! As I hear you share, it makes me wonder if one of your strengths is your intuition? You seem to be able to listen really well to your inner voice. (Criterion 1) In what ways could you listen to your inner voice more intentionally at your current job? (Criterion 2, Option A)

or

Of the careers you're considering, which ones would require intuitive thinking? (Criterion 2, Option B)

Example Response to Intermediate Client Statement 5

That's fantastic! Given your background in sales, I wonder if one of your skills might be in the area of persuading others; does that fit for you? (Criterion 1) In what ways could you use your influence more often in your current job? (Criterion 2, Option A)

or

Of all the careers you're currently considering, which ones in particular do you think would focus on persuading, influencing, or impacting others? (Criterion 2, Option B)

EXAMPLE RESPONSES TO ADVANCED-LEVEL CLIENT STATEMENTS FOR EXERCISE 1

Example Response to Advanced Client Statement 1

You know, as you share that, I get the sense that one of your strengths might be in your ability to plan! It sounds like a skill that's carried you far in the past. (Criterion 1) In what ways could you use your planning skills more with your current job? (Criterion 2, Option A)

or

In thinking about your top career options, which ones would benefit from a good planner? (Criterion 2, Option B)

Example Response to Advanced Client Statement 2

It sounds like you're really skilled at working with your hands and creating a tangible change for the better! (Criterion 1) How could you use this skill more in your current job? (Criterion 2, Option A)

or

If you'd like to explore this further, let's think through some careers that would allow you to create, fix, or build things. (Criterion 2, Option B)

Example Response to Advanced Client Statement 3

That's great! I hear many strengths as you share that story: your efficiency, reliability, and an ability to troubleshoot and solve some pretty complex problems. (Criterion 1) Given your strength in problem solving, how might you interface more with customers in need? (Criterion 2, Option A)

or

In thinking about careers you're considering now, which ones would pull on your strength in the area of troubleshooting and finding answers to complex problems? (Criterion 2, Option B)

Example Response to Advanced Client Statement 4

Baking! That's great! I hear a lot of skills embedded within that activity: perhaps being creative, being able to follow directions well, making something tangible. Do any of those resonate with you? (Criterion 1) In thinking about those general skills, how could you use more of them in your current career? (Criterion 2, Option A)

or

In thinking about those general skills, what career paths would allow you to use those skills on a regular basis? (Criterion 2, Option B)

Example Response to Advanced Client Statement 5

Very neat! Sounds like you have some strengths in public speaking and thinking on your feet. (Criterion 1) In what ways could you challenge yourself in your current job to talk more with the public and respond to issues as they're happening at work? (Criterion 2, Option A)

or

I wonder what careers might allow you to engage in more public speaking? (Criterion 2, Option B)

Exercise 2

Exploring Your Client's Values

Preparations for Exercise 2

1. Read the instructions in Chapter 2.
2. Download the Deliberate Practice Reaction Form and the Deliberate Practice Diary Form at https://www.apa.org/pubs/books/deliberate-practice-career-counseling (see the "Resources" tab; also available in Appendixes A and B, respectively).

Skill Description

Skill Difficulty Level: Beginner

When clients feel "stuck in a rut" at work, it is often an indication that their day-to-day career life may be misaligned with, or simply not capitalizing on, their most salient values. This exercise is designed to help you enter critical conversations with your clients about what is meaningful to them, how they make sense of their purpose, and how those values could be better aligned with their work.

The counselor should improvise a response to each client statement following these skill criteria:

1. **Reflect a value communicated by the client.** In this first skill criterion, the counselor highlights the value they hear embedded in what the client is sharing. Use your active listening skills to consider the underlying value, as values are not always explicitly stated by clients. This first step is essential because it ensures that you have adequately understood your client's salient values and because your client may not have considered values that are important to them before this exercise.

2. **Ask how the value could be more present in the client's current job or hobbies.** The next step is to invite your client to consider how they might honor their values further, either within their current job or within their avocations. Sometimes our clients' values

---

https://doi.org/10.1037/0000442-004
Deliberate Practice in Career Counseling, by J. M. Taylor, A. Vaz, and T. Rousmaniere
Copyright © 2025 by the American Psychological Association. All rights reserved.

align easily with their current jobs, but some values may be inconsistent with their current career, and a client may not have the privilege of easily shifting to another. In such cases, it is useful to facilitate a conversation with your client, exploring ways to engage in activities or values they are passionate about in their avocations or self-care hobbies outside of work.

> **SKILL CRITERIA FOR EXERCISE 2**
> 1. Reflect a value communicated by the client.
> 2. Ask how the value could be more present in the client's current job or hobbies.

Examples of Counselors Exploring Their Client's Values

Example 1

CLIENT: [*despondent*] I have three little boys, and I'm a single dad. I wish I had more time to spend with my children.

COUNSELOR: Spending time with your boys sounds really important. (Criterion 1) What do you think you could do to find greater work–life balance right now? For example, would your boss be open to a conversation about flexible work hours? (Criterion 2)

Example 2

CLIENT: [*nervous*] I saw someone yesterday who was asking for money on the street. I wished I could do more to help her.

COUNSELOR: It sounds like helping others and doing something good for them is important to you. (Criterion 1) How could you pursue your values of compassion and care for others more in your current job? (Criterion 2)

Example 3

CLIENT: [*angry*] Medication is so incredibly expensive in this country. It's so wrong that people can't get access to good health services and basic necessities whenever they need it.

COUNSELOR: It sounds like advocacy work may be close to your heart. (Criterion 1) In what ways could you stand up even more for others in your job or hobbies? (Criterion 2)

INSTRUCTIONS FOR EXERCISE 2

Step 1: Role-Play and Feedback

- The client says the first beginner client statement. The counselor **improvises** a response based on the skill criteria.
- The trainer (or, if not available, the client) provides **brief** feedback based on the skill criteria.
- The client then repeats the same statement, and the counselor again improvises a response. The trainer (or client) again provides brief feedback.

Step 2: Repeat

- Repeat Step 1 for all the statements **in the current difficulty level** (beginner, intermediate, or advanced).

Step 3: Assess and Adjust Difficulty

- The counselor completes the Deliberate Practice Reaction Form (see Appendix A) and decides whether to make the exercise easier or harder or to repeat the same difficulty level.

Step 4: Repeat for Approximately 15 Minutes

- Repeat Steps 1 to 3 for at least 15 minutes.
- The trainees then switch counselor and client roles and start over.

Now it's your turn! Follow Steps 1 and 2 from the instructions.

Remember: The goal of the role-play is for trainees to practice improvising responses to the client statements in a manner that (a) uses the skill criteria and (b) feels authentic for the trainee. **Example counselor responses for each client statement are provided at the end of this exercise. Trainees should attempt to improvise their own responses before reading the examples.**

BEGINNER-LEVEL CLIENT STATEMENTS FOR EXERCISE 2
Beginner Client Statement 1
[Lonely] I don't feel connected with anyone at work.
Beginner Client Statement 2
[Calm] On weekends, I love baking, and when the weather is nice, I love gardening. There's something so satisfying about seeing something come from nothing.
Beginner Client Statement 3
[Despondent] Right now my job feels so monotonous—I do the same things over and over. My schedule always looks the same, and I wish it wasn't that way.
Beginner Client Statement 4
[Regretful] I miss the autonomy of my old job. I used to be able to work from home on Fridays.
Beginner Client Statement 5
[Proud] I always try to come into work with a positive attitude. It just helps everyone have a bit better day.

 Assess and adjust the difficulty before moving to the next difficulty level (see Step 3 in the exercise instructions).

INTERMEDIATE-LEVEL CLIENT STATEMENTS FOR EXERCISE 2
Intermediate Client Statement 1
[Longing] I always looked up to my mother. She was so kind, gentle, and she treated everyone with respect.
Intermediate Client Statement 2
[Ashamed] My father lost his job when I was in high school, and we struggled for months to pay rent, put food on the table, and pay for his medical bills.
Intermediate Client Statement 3
[Frustrated] I worked so hard at my job for 5 years, and I never once was offered a raise or promotion!
Intermediate Client Statement 4
[Helpless] My last job was at a factory. I witnessed one of my coworkers have a traumatic injury from one of the machines. Now he is on permanent disability. I don't want that for me . . .
Intermediate Client Statement 5
[Tired] I'm finding work so boring. I wish I didn't feel so "stuck in a rut."

 Assess and adjust the difficulty before moving to the next difficulty level (see Step 3 in the exercise instructions).

ADVANCED-LEVEL CLIENT STATEMENTS FOR EXERCISE 2
Advanced Client Statement 1
[Discouraged] My last job was soooo boring. It was just too easy for me.
Advanced Client Statement 2
[Skeptical] I worked at a factory for the past 10 years. I hated working there. I always felt like someone was breathing down my back—like someone was always watching me.
Advanced Client Statement 3
[Despondent] I'm often the only Black woman in the boardrooms. I wish I had mentors who looked like me.
Advanced Client Statement 4
[Remorseful] I really miss living in Florida! The sunshine, palm trees, and ocean breeze used to greet me every morning. I just felt so much calmer there.
Advanced Client Statement 5
[Insecure] I moved to Utah to support my partner, but I really miss my old job. I really felt like I was part of a team.

> **Assess and adjust the difficulty here (see Step 3 in the exercise instructions). If appropriate, follow the instructions to make the exercise even more challenging (see Appendix A).**

Example Counselor Responses: Exploring Your Client's Values

Remember: Trainees should attempt to improvise their own responses before reading the examples. **Do not read the following responses verbatim unless you are having trouble coming up with your own!**

EXAMPLE RESPONSES TO BEGINNER-LEVEL CLIENT STATEMENTS FOR EXERCISE 2
Example Response to Beginner Client Statement 1
It sounds like connection is really important to you. (Criterion 1) What sorts of things could you do to build community with your coworkers? (Criterion 2)
Example Response to Beginner Client Statement 2
I hear how much you value creating things and seeing them blossom! (Criterion 1) I wonder how you might infuse more creativity in your current job? (Criterion 2)
Example Response to Beginner Client Statement 3
It sounds like variety is important to you. (Criterion 1) I wonder if there are any specific ways you might break up your workday and vary your activities a bit more? And if that doesn't seem feasible, I wonder in what ways you might infuse more variety in your schedule outside of work? (Criterion 2)
Example Response to Beginner Client Statement 4
It sounds like autonomy is important to you. (Criterion 1) If you don't have much autonomy at work, what could you do more intentionally during your off hours to enjoy the things you love the most? (Criterion 2)
Example Response to Beginner Client Statement 5
It sounds like promoting positivity in the workplace is an important value of yours. (Criterion 1) What might be some ways you could more intentionally infuse your positive attitude into your work? (Criterion 2)

EXAMPLE RESPONSES TO INTERMEDIATE-LEVEL CLIENT STATEMENTS FOR EXERCISE 2

Example Response to Intermediate Client Statement 1

She sounds like an incredible person! And I can hear that her kindness and respect for others are values you also seem to hold dear. (Criterion 1) I wonder, in what ways might you honor her kindness in your own daily work? (Criterion 2)

Example Response to Intermediate Client Statement 2

I imagine that was really stressful. I take it that financial security is of real value to you, especially after what you've been through. (Criterion 1) What would you need in your current job to feel stable and secure? (Criterion 2)

Example Response to Intermediate Client Statement 3

Yeah, totally! I hear your frustration. It sounds like opportunities for advancement at work are important to you. (Criterion 1) What could you do to increase the likelihood of getting a promotion or advancement at work? (Criterion 2)

Example Response to Intermediate Client Statement 4

Wow, that sounds scary! I gather from what you've shared that it's really important that you feel safe in your workplace. (Criterion 1) What things could you do to feel safe in your current job? (Criterion 2)

Example Response to Intermediate Client Statement 5

It sounds like you really want to be engaged in your work. (Criterion 1) What would make your current job feel more exciting or interesting? (Criterion 2)

EXAMPLE RESPONSES TO ADVANCED-LEVEL CLIENT STATEMENTS FOR EXERCISE 2

Example Response to Advanced Client Statement 1

Oof! I imagine it was hard to stay motivated in a job you found boring. And it sounds like you really value feeling engaged and challenged in what you do. (Criterion 1) In what ways do you want a job to challenge you? (Criterion 2)

Example Response to Advanced Client Statement 2

It sounds like you felt micromanaged in your last job and that freedom to work autonomously is something you value. (Criterion 1) In what ways could you hold more autonomy in your career or in other areas of your life? (Criterion 2)

Example Response to Advanced Client Statement 3

I hear that connection, community, and representation are really important to you. (Criterion 1) In what ways could you connect with other Black leaders in your field? Perhaps at conferences? In professional organizations? Somewhere else? (Criterion 2)

Example Response to Advanced Client Statement 4

It sounds like the peace you found when you lived in Florida is really important to you. (Criterion 1) In what ways could you bring more peace and sunshine to your current job? (Criterion 2)

Example Response to Advanced Client Statement 5

I wonder if you've been feeling a bit lonely since the move? And that connection and community are of real importance to you? (Criterion 1) How might you foster more connection and community with others in your new job? (Criterion 2)

Exercise 3

Exploring Your Client's Decision-Making Styles

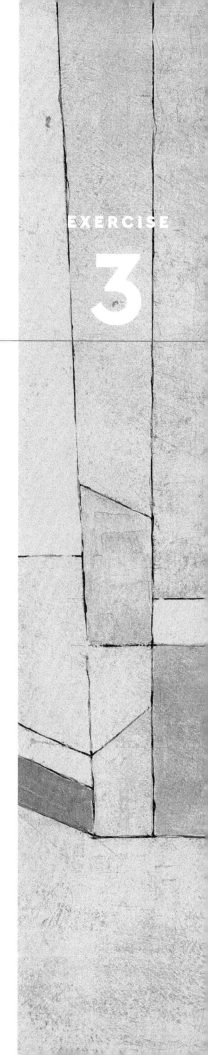

Preparations for Exercise 3

1. Read the instructions in Chapter 2.
2. Download the Deliberate Practice Reaction Form and the Deliberate Practice Diary Form at https://www.apa.org/pubs/books/deliberate-practice-career-counseling (see the "Resources" tab; also available in Appendixes A and B, respectively).

Skill Description

Skill Difficulty Level: Beginner

Career indecision represents a key issue that many career counseling clients face (Gati & Levin, 2014). In fact, some clients may turn to career counselors to tell them what to do. It is important for you to resist the temptation to prescribe career plans for your clients and instead work with your clients to explore what holds them back from making a career decision. By practicing this skill, you will learn techniques to support your clients in self-discovery and empower them toward future action.

This skill offers counselors an instrumental tool to support clients who are feeling "stuck" and unable to move forward with the next step of their career planning process. In this exercise, you will explore your client's indecision, the strategies they have tried thus far to reach a decision, and ideas for further exploration.

Keep in mind that clients may be indecisive for many reasons. Some clients are indecisive because they have rarely, or never, made important decisions by themselves or lack self-efficacy around the decision-making process (Bullock-Yowell et al., 2014; Udayar et al., 2020). Some clients are indecisive because they are struggling between many potentially good solutions and feel pressure to choose "the right one" (see also Storme et al., 2019). Likewise, some clients are indecisive because they do not know enough about particular career paths to make a decision between different options

---

https://doi.org/10.1037/0000442-005
Deliberate Practice in Career Counseling, by J. M. Taylor, A. Vaz, and T. Rousmaniere
Copyright © 2025 by the American Psychological Association. All rights reserved.

and are feeling pressured or anxious about making a career path decision, a finding observed across a range of cultures (Roche et al., 2017; Xu & Bhang, 2019). These are just a few reasons why clients sometimes struggle to make career decisions.

To use this skill, the counselor should improvise a response to each client statement following these skill criteria:

1. **Explore what the client has done in the past in an attempt to resolve their indecision.** The goal of this first step is to ensure the client feels heard and understood before exploring the client's decision-making process further. Information uncovered in this step also allows the counselor further insight into the client's decision-making process and what they have tried thus far to reach career decision clarity. For the purposes of this practice, the counselor should fulfill this step and immediately move on to the next criterion; however, in a real career counseling session this first step can take several back-and-forths between client and counselor before moving on to Criterion 2.

2. **Invite collaboration to brainstorm by tentatively suggesting a task to address the client's uncertainty.** This second step moves the counselor and client from exploration to action. In this step, the counselor will offer a suggestion in the form of an activity or assessment to support the career decision-making process, or the counselor will invite the client to nominate a course of action to gain greater career clarity.

Importantly, any suggestion provided should be tentative and open to the client's feedback. Depending on the current issue a client is experiencing, suggestions might include the following:

- Taking coursework or continuing education in an area of interest.
- Conducting an informational interview with someone who is in a career path of interest.
- Learning more about a specific career path through resources, such as the Occupational Outlook Handbook (U.S. Bureau of Labor Statistics, 2024).
- Inviting the client to engage in relevant career assessment tools (e.g., interest inventory, values card sort).

SKILL CRITERIA FOR EXERCISE 3

1. Explore what the client has done in the past in an attempt to resolve their indecision.
2. Invite collaboration to brainstorm by tentatively suggesting a task to address the client's uncertainty.

Examples of Counselors Exploring Decision-Making Styles

Example 1

CLIENT: [*anxious*] I wish I could figure out what I want to do with the rest of my life. I'm getting pressure from my academic advisor to decide on a major, and I just . . . I just don't know how to decide!

COUNSELOR: I hear how stressful this has been! What have you tried so far to explore what major you're interested in? (Criterion 1) Have you considered interviewing seniors in different majors? What are your thoughts about starting there to learn more about their experiences? (Criterion 2)

Example 2

CLIENT: [*hopeless*] I should know what I want to do with my career by now. I just know I'm not happy.

COUNSELOR: I hear the pressure you're feeling to make a decision. Let's start by exploring what you've tried so far to get a better sense of career paths that might make you happy. How have you explored career options so far? (Criterion 1) Oftentimes, happiness or joy is linked with a felt sense of meaning in what we do. How would you feel about us starting with a few assessments to explore careers that align with your interests and values—careers that may capitalize on your greater meaning and purpose? (Criterion 2)

Example 3

CLIENT: [*stressed*] How should I know what I want to do? I don't even know what I want to eat for lunch!

COUNSELOR: I imagine this whole process has felt really stressful and confusing. What have you attempted so far to explore career options? (Criterion 1) How would you feel about us starting by learning a bit more about who you are, especially your main interests and values, as that may give us ideas about career paths that may be a good fit for you? (Criterion 2)

INSTRUCTIONS FOR EXERCISE 3

Step 1: Role-Play and Feedback

- The client says the first beginner client statement. The counselor **improvises** a response based on the skill criteria.
- The trainer (or, if not available, the client) provides **brief** feedback based on the skill criteria.
- The client then repeats the same statement, and the counselor again improvises a response. The trainer (or client) again provides brief feedback.

Step 2: Repeat

- Repeat Step 1 for all the statements **in the current difficulty level** (beginner, intermediate, or advanced).

Step 3: Assess and Adjust Difficulty

- The counselor completes the Deliberate Practice Reaction Form (see Appendix A) and decides whether to make the exercise easier or harder or to repeat the same difficulty level.

Step 4: Repeat for Approximately 15 Minutes

- Repeat Steps 1 to 3 for at least 15 minutes.
- The trainees then switch counselor and client roles and start over.

Now it's your turn! Follow Steps 1 and 2 from the instructions.

Remember: The goal of the role-play is for trainees to practice improvising responses to the client statements in a manner that (a) uses the skill criteria and (b) feels authentic for the trainee. **Example counselor responses for each client statement are provided at the end of this exercise. Trainees should attempt to improvise their own responses before reading the examples.**

BEGINNER-LEVEL CLIENT STATEMENTS FOR EXERCISE 3
Beginner Client Statement 1
[**Frustrated**] I've considered a career as an architect, but I'm also thinking about a career in law. I just don't know what to choose!
Beginner Client Statement 2
[**Hopeless**] I've lost "it." I just don't find anything in work meaningful anymore. I don't know what to do.
Beginner Client Statement 3
[**Embarrassed**] I just don't know what to do . . . I'm failing all of my pre-med classes. Maybe I'm just not cut out for this.
Beginner Client Statement 4
[**Confused**] I just don't find the field of law exciting anymore. I don't know . . . maybe I'm overthinking it, but maybe this is a sign that I should pursue something else.
Beginner Client Statement 5
[**Conflicted**] My boss is insufferable. Every day I dread going to work. But I have to provide for my family. I just don't know what to do next.

 Assess and adjust the difficulty before moving to the next difficulty level (see Step 3 in the exercise instructions).

INTERMEDIATE-LEVEL CLIENT STATEMENTS FOR EXERCISE 3
Intermediate Client Statement 1
[Frustrated] All of my friends know what they want to major in . . . but I have no idea! There are too many options.
Intermediate Client Statement 2
[Remorseful] My degree is in engineering, but I've always had a passion for law. I'm graduating from college next month, and I just don't know what to do. I feel so conflicted.
Intermediate Client Statement 3
[Stressed] I've been thinking about going back to school, but I just can't decide if the timing is right for me. Between working full time and caring for my parents, I have so much on my plate.
Intermediate Client Statement 4
[Discouraged] I was never really passionate about my job at the bank. I just worked there so I could earn a living. Now that I'm older, I want to pursue a job I'm passionate about . . . but I don't even know what that job would look like.
Intermediate Client Statement 5
[Inadequate] Everyone else in class seems to "get it," but I'm struggling in all my computer science classes. I've even hired tutors, and nothing is helping. Maybe I'm not cut out for this.

 Assess and adjust the difficulty before moving to the next difficulty level (see Step 3 in the exercise instructions).

ADVANCED-LEVEL CLIENT STATEMENTS FOR EXERCISE 3
Advanced Client Statement 1
[**Downtrodden**] My parents want me to go into medicine, but it just doesn't feel "right" to me. I don't know . . . maybe I should just go into pre-med.
Advanced Client Statement 2
[**Overwhelmed**] I'm balancing a full-time job and life as a single dad while also taking care of my mother who was diagnosed with cancer last year. I don't know how much longer I can do this. Something has to change.
Advanced Client Statement 3
[**Insecure**] I started my job at the factory a few months ago and got my first term evaluation. My manager told me I'm not measuring up. I don't know . . . maybe I'm just not meant to do this job. I'm just not good enough.
Advanced Client Statement 4
[**Angry and rageful**] My boss fired me from my job this week. I can't even believe it! My wife's birthday is tomorrow—how do I tell her I don't even have a job now? At this point, I don't even know what other jobs I'd go for!
Advanced Client Statement 5
[**Conflicted**] My wife and I just had our first child. I've been thinking about quitting so I can spend more time with the baby, but I'm worried my wife and I won't be able to support our family if I quit. But if I don't quit, we'd have to figure out how to gather enough savings to pay for a nanny. I don't know what to do!

 Assess and adjust the difficulty here (see Step 3 in the exercise instructions). If appropriate, follow the instructions to make the exercise even more challenging (see Appendix A).

Example Counselor Responses: Exploring Decision-Making Styles

Remember: Trainees should attempt to improvise their own responses before reading the examples. **Do not read the following responses verbatim unless you are having trouble coming up with your own responses!**

EXAMPLE RESPONSES TO BEGINNER-LEVEL CLIENT STATEMENTS FOR EXERCISE 3
Example Response to Beginner Client Statement 1
I hear how hard this process has been. What have you done so far to learn more about careers in architecture and law? (Criterion 1) Why don't we start by exploring the educational requirements, work environments, daily tasks, job outlook, and pay for both careers? (Criterion 2)
Example Response to Beginner Client Statement 2
I hear the sadness in your voice. You want a career that matches your calling, but it feels misaligned. What have you tried so far to find meaning in your work? (Criterion 1) How would you feel about us starting by exploring your calling further? (Criterion 2)
Example Response to Beginner Client Statement 3
It sounds like your classes have been very stressful. How did you decide on your pre-med major? (Criterion 1) Why don't we start by exploring what attracted you to medicine and learn more about your interests and values? From there, perhaps we can explore related careers that capitalize on what you like about medicine as well. (Criterion 2)
Example Response to Beginner Client Statement 4
I hear that you're feeling really conflicted. How did you decide on a career in law in the first place? (Criterion 1) Let's start by exploring your earliest passions, values, and interests in law. From there, perhaps we can explore what an "exciting" career might look like and consider ways to infuse more excitement in your current job, your hobbies/avocations, or, perhaps, another career path. (Criterion 2)
Example Response to Beginner Client Statement 5
I imagine it's been really difficult to work with a boss who is so challenging. I can see you're feeling conflicted about your job because it does provide some security for your family. When you decided to apply for this job, what were the primary motivating factors for you in choosing this job? (Criterion 1) Why don't we start by exploring your "must haves" in a career? This might include good colleagues and financial stability. From there, we can explore ways to deal with challenging colleagues or perhaps we can also explore other career options or other companies in your field. (Criterion 2)

EXAMPLE RESPONSES TO INTERMEDIATE-LEVEL CLIENT STATEMENTS FOR EXERCISE 3

Example Response to Intermediate Client Statement 1

It sounds like it feels really confusing and overwhelming to choose a major. What have you tried so far to figure it out? (Criterion 1) Let's start by exploring your favorite classes and what it is about particular subjects you like. How does that sound? (Criterion 2)

Example Response to Intermediate Client Statement 2

I hear how difficult this has been. What have you tried so far to explore your career options? (Criterion 1) Perhaps we could start by exploring your interests in engineering and law. Let's look at where those interests overlap and where they differ, next we can explore career paths that might combine your underlying interests, and then let's see where that takes us. How would you feel about us starting there? (Criterion 2)

Example Response to Intermediate Client Statement 3

It sounds like you've been feeling overwhelmed, yet there's also a part of your heart that feels drawn to getting more education. As you look back at other decisions you've made in the past, how have you decided if the timing was right? (Criterion 1) Perhaps we can start by exploring what your other responsibilities and obligations are right now, along with ways to prioritize things, to see if you have the time and space for school at this stage of your life. (Criterion 2)

Example Response to Intermediate Client Statement 4

It sounds like you've been really thinking about what you want in a career and what it might mean to find a career that's meaningful to you. What have you tried so far to explore career paths you're passionate about? (Criterion 1) Because you want to find a job that's a passion for you, let's start by delving into your values. How would you feel about starting there? (Criterion 2)

Example Response to Intermediate Client Statement 5

I hear that you're feeling like you're not measuring up in your classes and are questioning if computer science is right for you. What have you done so far to explore your strengths? (Criterion 1) Let's start by exploring your strengths further and then brainstorm how you might build on those strengths for your future career path. How does that sound? (Criterion 2)

EXAMPLE RESPONSES TO ADVANCED-LEVEL CLIENT STATEMENTS FOR EXERCISE 3

Example Response to Advanced Client Statement 1

It sounds like you're being strongly encouraged to pursue medicine, but your intuition is telling you otherwise. How have you wrestled through decisions in the past when your wishes differ from your parents? (Criterion 1) Perhaps we can start by exploring your values and your parents' values. Would you be interested in making space to explore the ways in which your values are similar to or different from your parents? (Criterion 2)

Example Response to Advanced Client Statement 2

I hear that you're feeling pulled in a lot of directions and are feeling really stressed. What have you tried thus far to manage this load and create less stress and more satisfaction with your job? (Criterion 1) Why don't we start by exploring what a typical day is like for you? From there, we can brainstorm ways to create more balance—either within your current job, in your home life, or perhaps with new job possibilities. (Criterion 2)

Example Response to Advanced Client Statement 3

It sounds like the evaluation process was really discouraging. It's even made you question whether this job is for you. When you first decided on this job, how did you make that decision? (Criterion 1) Perhaps we can start by exploring the challenges and barriers you're currently facing with your job. Let's also examine further the messages you've been telling yourself and the goals you have for your job. (Criterion 2)

Example Response to Advanced Client Statement 4

Talk about timing! I imagine this must be extremely stressful, frustrating, and scary. It's even more stressful when we can't imagine other job possibilities and don't know where to turn next. So, let's start by exploring that further: What have you done so far to explore jobs that might interest you? (Criterion 1) Perhaps we can start by exploring your skill set and consider jobs that align well with your strengths. Then we can explore careers that map onto those strengths well. (Criterion 2)

Example Response to Advanced Client Statement 5

I know it's a complicated decision, with benefits and drawbacks attached to either quitting or remaining at your job. . . . How much do you know, at this point, about how your finances would be impacted by your decision to stay in your current job and hire a nanny or quit? (Criterion 1) From a practical standpoint, perhaps we can start by exploring what you see as the benefits and drawbacks of each decision, why you feel pulled toward each option, and what your finances may look like as a result of each decision. How would you feel about us starting there? (Criterion 2)

Exercise 4

Exploring Your Client's Cultural and Familial Influences

Preparations for Exercise 4

1. Read the instructions in Chapter 2.

2. Download the Deliberate Practice Reaction Form and the Deliberate Practice Diary Form at https://www.apa.org/pubs/books/deliberate-practice-career-counseling (see the "Resources" tab; also available in Appendixes A and B, respectively).

Skill Description

Skill Difficulty Level: Intermediate

One critical component of career counseling involves attending to the intersectional identities of both the client and the counselor and how familial and cultural values impact the client's career impressions and decisions. Exploring the messages and assumptions held around specific careers can give career counselors a window into the values placed on a range of careers. In this exercise, we practice strategies to help your client delve into the impact and influence of familial and cultural messages they have received around a range of careers they may be considering or eliminating. Exploring career-related values can assist clients in processing the influences of others and the clients' worldviews, honoring their cultural values, and assisting clients in providing greater clarity on their career interests, options, and decisions (Flores & Bike, 2014).

At a foundational level, career counselors should explore the influence of a salient culture or family value related to careers. A more advanced version of this involves exploring the influences of intersectional identities clients hold related to careers. For example, rather than simply asking a client about how her identity as a woman or how her identity as a person of color impacts her career decisions, a career counselor could instead explore the combined impact of both identities on her career decisions. Both identities likely impact the client's career decisions, and this influence is rarely

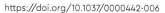

https://doi.org/10.1037/0000442-006
Deliberate Practice in Career Counseling, by J. M. Taylor, A. Vaz, and T. Rousmaniere
Copyright © 2025 by the American Psychological Association. All rights reserved.

unidimensional. Exploring a client's layered identities can be particularly helpful in exploring multicultural influences in a more nuanced way. For additional multicultural counseling skills relevant to career counseling, please refer to *Deliberate Practice in Multicultural Therapy* (Harris et al., 2024).

Some career counseling clients will find exploring their cultural identities and their influence on their careers a relatively easy exercise, but for many, particularly clients from dominant cultures and/or those who are less familiar with their cultural lineages, this exercise may be initially challenging. Indeed, you may be met with a look of confusion when you ask clients about cultures salient to them. In cases like this, we encourage you to start by inviting the client to talk about messages they received, implicitly or explicitly, from family members about particular careers or the value of careers more generally. You might also consider messages clients received around careers "appropriate" for employees with regard to their gender, their geographic location (e.g., urban, rural, suburban), their religion, their socioeconomic status, or their political ideologies. Of course, messages clients have received related to their ethnic or racial identity can also be useful to explore.

Using this skill set, the counselor should improvise a response to each client statement following these skill criteria:

1. **Paraphrase the client's statement.** We encourage you to begin this exercise by first restating what your client shared with you. This is important for three reasons: (a) It will help to ensure you appropriately understand what your client shared; (b) it is often useful for clients to hear, through another's voice, what they've communicated with you; and (c) it will provide you with an opportunity to consider what the client shared before asking a follow-up question about specific cultural or familial influences.

2. **On the basis of the client's statement, ask an open-ended question about cultural or familial messages the client may have received.** Asking an open-ended question will allow your client space to explore, from perspectives salient for them, the messages and impact of particular cultures and/or family influences on their career decisions, assumptions, biases, pressures, and values.

SKILL CRITERIA FOR EXERCISE 4

1. Paraphrase the client's statement.
2. On the basis of the client's statement, ask an open-ended question about the cultural or familial messages the client may have received.

Examples of Counselors Exploring Cultural and Familial Influences

Example 1

CLIENT: [*overwhelmed*] My family always worked hard. I work hard too, but I'm just so, so . . . tired. A part of me wishes I could take a break.

COUNSELOR: I understand that hard work is an important family value, and I also understand that at the same time, you're feeling exhausted. (Criterion 1) What messages have you received from your family about resting? (Criterion 2)

Example 2

CLIENT: [*despondent*] I feel like my job is such a disappointment. I just want to make my family proud.

COUNSELOR: It sounds like it's important to you to pursue a career that would honor your family. (Criterion 1) What are some qualities in careers that are important in your family? (Criterion 2)

Example 3

CLIENT: [*stressed*] In my culture, I was taught to take care of myself first so that no one else has to take care of me. I gotta get myself together so I can then take care of others.

COUNSELOR: From what I gather, you don't want to be a burden to others and having some stability in your life will enable you to then help others along the way. (Criterion 1) How has your culture's value of self-reliance influenced the way you approach work? (Criterion 2)

INSTRUCTIONS FOR EXERCISE 4

Step 1: Role-Play and Feedback

- The client says the first beginner client statement. The counselor **improvises** a response based on the skill criteria.
- The trainer (or, if not available, the client) provides **brief** feedback based on the skill criteria.
- The client then repeats the same statement, and the counselor again improvises a response. The trainer (or client) again provides brief feedback.

Step 2: Repeat

- Repeat Step 1 for all the statements **in the current difficulty level** (beginner, intermediate, or advanced).

Step 3: Assess and Adjust Difficulty

- The counselor completes the Deliberate Practice Reaction Form (see Appendix A) and decides whether to make the exercise easier or harder or to repeat the same difficulty level.

Step 4: Repeat for Approximately 15 Minutes

- Repeat Steps 1 to 3 for at least 15 minutes.
- The trainees then switch counselor and client roles and start over.

Now it's your turn! Follow Steps 1 and 2 from the instructions.

Remember: The goal of the role-play is for trainees to practice improvising responses to the client statements in a manner that (a) uses the skill criteria and (b) feels authentic for the trainee. **Example counselor responses for each client statement are provided at the end of this exercise. Trainees should attempt to improvise their own responses before reading the examples.**

BEGINNER-LEVEL CLIENT STATEMENTS FOR EXERCISE 4
Beginner Client Statement 1
[Downtrodden] I'd love to be a ski instructor . . . but I know my parents wouldn't be okay with me just doing a seasonal job.
Beginner Client Statement 2
[Conflicted] I was running a multimillion-dollar company until the economy crashed. Now I don't know how I'll provide for my family.
Beginner Client Statement 3
[Exhausted] I've spent my whole life caring for others in my family. After all, it's an important value in my culture. But I'm just so . . . tired.
Beginner Client Statement 4
[Stressed] I told my family I plan to major in art. Their first question was, "How will you support a family with an art degree?"
Beginner Client Statement 5
[Matter of factly] My parents always told me that whatever career I pursue, make sure it's a good one that won't make me a burden to others. In my culture, we're taught not to be trouble to anyone.

> **Assess and adjust the difficulty before moving to the next difficulty level (see Step 3 in the exercise instructions).**

INTERMEDIATE-LEVEL CLIENT STATEMENTS FOR EXERCISE 4
Intermediate Client Statement 1
[Insecure] New York City is fast-paced. You have to hustle to get ahead. It was such a shock to move here from my small town of Bloomington, Indiana. I never quite feel like I'm measuring up.
Intermediate Client Statement 2
[Anxious] This is my second year in law school, and I've gotta figure out a way to do a better job than others in my cohort so I can rank higher in the program.
Intermediate Client Statement 3
[Overwhelmed] I've had to hustle my whole life. My family and I grew up in a trailer park. Most people from my neighborhood never made it out of our tiny town. When I tell my hometown friends that I got a scholarship so I could attend college, they looked at me like I disowned them—like we can no longer relate. I feel so disconnected from my hometown.
Intermediate Client Statement 4
[Firmly] In the military, I was taught to value structure and organization.
Intermediate Client Statement 5
[Embarrassed] The religion I was raised in says that people should be humble and not strive for material wealth . . . but I'm tired of being broke and want to have a career that makes a lot of money.

 Assess and adjust the difficulty before moving to the next difficulty level (see Step 3 in the exercise instructions).

ADVANCED-LEVEL CLIENT STATEMENTS FOR EXERCISE 4
Advanced Client Statement 1
[Hesitant] My partner wants me to stay at home with the kids. I know he expects me to do this, but I've always wanted to be an interior designer.
Advanced Client Statement 2
[Exasperated] I'm supposed to be the "breadwinner" in our relationship, after all. But I lost my job, and I feel like I lost a piece of myself.
Advanced Client Statement 3
[Inadequate] My parents raised me with a cultural value to work hard to honor my family and the sacrifices they made for me to get here. I just hope I measure up.
Advanced Client Statement 4
[Discouraged] I am attending college later in life. I look at my classmates and feel like I don't belong. I feel like I'm 20 years late to life.
Advanced Client Statement 5
[Disgust] Are you actually asking if I should be a nurse?! My parents insist that I pursue a very high-status career like doctor or lawyer. They would drop dead if I told them I was thinking about that!

> **Assess and adjust the difficulty here (see Step 3 in the exercise instructions). If appropriate, follow the instructions to make the exercise even more challenging (see Appendix A).**

Example Counselor Responses: Exploring Cultural and Familial Influences

Remember: Trainees should attempt to improvise their own responses before reading the examples. **Do not read the following responses verbatim unless you are having trouble coming up with your own!**

EXAMPLE RESPONSES TO BEGINNER-LEVEL CLIENT STATEMENTS FOR EXERCISE 4
Example Response to Beginner Client Statement 1
It seems that finding a stable career is an important value to your parents. (Criterion 1) What messages have you received about "seasonal work" from your family or from others in your cultural circles? (Criterion 2)
Example Response to Beginner Client Statement 2
I understand that providing some stability and security for your family is important to you. (Criterion 1) What sort of messages have you received about providing for your family, and how is that impacting your career decisions now? (Criterion 2)
Example Response to Beginner Client Statement 3
I sense that helping others is an important value within your culture. I also understand that you are feeling really exhausted and very burned out. (Criterion 1) Because caring for others is important in your culture, how might feeling burned out impact your ability to care for others, and in what ways might you also take care of yourself in the process? (Criterion 2)
Example Response to Beginner Client Statement 4
Oof! I gather that there is a lot of pressure wrapped up in your choice of a major and its ability to provide for a family. (Criterion 1) How does the pressure to provide for your family impact your satisfaction with your art internship right now and your current art projects? (Criterion 2)
Example Response to Beginner Client Statement 5
It seems like one message you've received is that you shouldn't be another's obligation. (Criterion 1) How does that message of "not burdening others" impact your career decisions now? (Criterion 2)

EXAMPLE RESPONSES TO INTERMEDIATE-LEVEL CLIENT STATEMENTS FOR EXERCISE 4

Example Response to Intermediate Client Statement 1

It seems like the fast-paced culture in New York City doesn't align with values from your hometown and has made you question if you measure up. (Criterion 1) What messages did you receive from your hometown about what it means to "measure up"? (Criterion 2)

Example Response to Intermediate Client Statement 2

I'm getting that there's a lot of competition in your law school and pressure to rank highly. (Criterion 1) Where did your messages about competition and success stem from? (Criterion 2)

Example Response to Intermediate Client Statement 3

I sense that you're feeling really detached from those you were close to in your town. (Criterion 1) What expectations do people from your hometown hold about appropriate career paths, and how do those expectations impact how you are currently approaching your experience in college now? (Criterion 2)

Example Response to Intermediate Client Statement 4

I see. Order and organization are important values embedded in the military culture. (Criterion 1) How do those values impact your current choice in career paths? (Criterion 2)

Example Response to Intermediate Client Statement 5

It seems like there is some conflict between the religion you were raised in and your career ambitions. (Criterion 1) Can we explore the messages you received growing up and how they conflict with your goals? (Criterion 2)

EXAMPLE RESPONSES TO ADVANCED-LEVEL CLIENT STATEMENTS FOR EXERCISE 4

Example Response to Advanced Client Statement 1

It sounds like you're feeling pulled in two directions: either taking care of your children at home or choosing a career path you've longed for in interior design. (Criterion 1) In what ways might those two values, caretaking and a career path, not necessarily be mutually exclusive? (Criterion 2)

Example Response to Advanced Client Statement 2

I sense the tension and stress you're experiencing; you've lost your job and you've been facing a lot of pressure not being able to support your family financially given the job loss. (Criterion 1) Let's talk more about expectations and how they are impacting you now. What other messages have you received about expectations in your relationship? (Criterion 2)

Example Response to Advanced Client Statement 3

I recognize you want to honor your family and their hard work in getting you to where you are today. Given their sacrifices, it sounds like there's a fear you hold that you may not be doing "enough"—that you may be inadequate. (Criterion 1) As you think about the cultural messages you've received, what would it mean to "measure up"? (Criterion 2)

Example Response to Advanced Client Statement 4

It sounds like college has been an isolating experience and has made you question your timing in pursuing a college degree. (Criterion 1) What messages have you received about being a college student and from whom? (Criterion 2)

Example Response to Advanced Client Statement 5

I understand that pursuing a career in nursing feels really incongruent with what your parents expect. (Criterion 1) What other messages did you hear from your parents about their expectations for your career? Would you like to explore the intersection of your career goals and your parents' expectations? (Criterion 2)

EXERCISE 5

Discussing the Benefits of Career Counseling

Preparations for Exercise 5

1. Read the instructions in Chapter 2.

2. Download the Deliberate Practice Reaction Form and the Deliberate Practice Diary Form at https://www.apa.org/pubs/books/deliberate-practice-career-counseling (see the "Resources" tab; also available in Appendixes A and B, respectively).

Skill Description

Skill Difficulty Level: Intermediate

Clients may pursue career counseling for a range of reasons. Some may visit your office on their own volition—they are currently unsatisfied in their career, they have experienced career transitions, they are considering retirement or a shift in their career, they question their career path or want to explore a college major or technical training, they are struggling with coworkers or a boss, they want to learn more about themselves, they want to set goals for the future—this list could continue! However, others may engage in career counseling because someone encouraged them to visit you—a partner, a parent, an academic advisor, or a mentor. In these cases, your client may be hesitant about the benefits of career counseling and unsure of its usefulness. Even when the client proactively pursues career counseling, they may still question if it will really be beneficial for them and if it is worth the investment—both in time and, potentially, money.

This exercise will help you learn how to explain the benefits of engaging in career counseling that are relevant to your client's concerns. Clients can derive a range of benefits from career counseling, including gaining deeper insights and clarity regarding their career goals, interests, skill set, and understanding the impact of career messages they have received on their decision-making process. Included in the skill criteria box for this exercise is a list of ways clients often benefit from career counseling, but consider this as just a starting point and feel free to add your own thoughts to this list as well.

https://doi.org/10.1037/0000442-007

Deliberate Practice in Career Counseling, by J. M. Taylor, A. Vaz, and T. Rousmaniere
Copyright © 2025 by the American Psychological Association. All rights reserved.

Keeping this in mind, the counselor should improvise a response to each of the client statements following these skill criteria:

1. **Give a rationale regarding why career counseling might help address the client's concerns.** Begin by providing a direct reason as to why career counseling may benefit your client. This can help them "buy into" career counseling and stay engaged in the process. As with any type of counseling, good listening skills are a must. Listen carefully for their concerns and their needs, and tailor your rationale in response to those concerns and needs. If they have not noted any specific concerns that brought them to career counseling (e.g., "My mom thinks it would help"), start by noting some common reasons why others have tried career counseling. Keep in mind that providing rationales for the benefits of career counseling is not about challenging or arguing with your client. The purpose here really is to "plant a seed"—to suggest some reasons why career counseling could be useful for them to consider. The purpose is not to convince your client that they should engage in career counseling.

2. **Practice verbal fluency: Keep rationales clear, articulate, and not too long.** Aim to provide direct and concise responses rather than providing verbose rationales for career counseling. Long responses may come across to your client as defensive responses. Focus as much as you can on answering their questions directly and opening space for them to share.

3. **Check with the client on their reactions to the provided rationale.** After sharing one reason why career counseling could support them, invite your client to share their thoughts and reactions to your rationale. This will allow you to gain deeper insight into your client's objectives, areas they wish to address and explore, and their priorities and goals for career counseling. Inviting your client to share also reinforces the idea that you are a collaborative team. You will provide career counseling support, but your client is the ultimate expert on themselves, and checking in with them ensures that you are aligned with them in your approach.

SKILL CRITERIA FOR EXERCISE 5

1. Give a rationale regarding why career counseling might help address the client's concerns. Common themes for rationales to discuss with clients include the following:
    - Engaging in self-exploration (e.g., exploring what the client desires to achieve out of their education, career, and life).
    - Discussing concerns, goals, desires and feelings surrounding the client's training, career choices, or career transitions.
    - Understanding how the client's cultures, family, interests, values, and skills may impact their career development and decisions (refer back to the exploration skills from Exercises 1 through 4).
    - Providing resources and skills relevant to the client's career development, planning, and a range of potential career paths.
    - Assisting the client in working through and responding to changes in their career (e.g., career transitions, retirements, new roles).
2. Practice verbal fluency: Keep rationales clear, articulate, and not too long.
3. Check with the client on their reactions to the provided rationale.

Examples of Discussing the Benefits of Career Counseling

Example 1

CLIENT: [*curious*] My mom told me to come see you because I'm failing in my current major. But how can you really help me?

COUNSELOR: Great question! I think there are several things we could do together to help you out. One of the things we can do together is explore your interests, skills, and values to find a major that's a good fit for you. (Criteria 1 and 2) How would you feel about us starting there? (Criterion 3)

Example 2

CLIENT: [*defeated*] I really don't know if career counseling is worth it. I know I need to figure out a better solution to deal with my abusive supervisor, but I don't really think anything will ever change.

COUNSELOR: A few things we could explore in career counseling together could be skills to advocate for yourself, boundaries with your supervisor at work, and allies to support you in the process. (Criteria 1 and 2) Would that be something of interest to you? (Criterion 3)

Example 3

CLIENT: [*skeptical*] recently lost my job, and there has been a lot of tension in my relationship with my wife. I tried couples counseling, and I didn't find it helpful. Why would career counseling be any different?

COUNSELOR: People find career counseling useful for a range of reasons. Given that you recently lost your job, a few of the things we can explore are practical ways to respond to that change and prepare for a new job. (Criteria 1 and 2) Would that feel useful to you? (Criterion 3)

INSTRUCTIONS FOR EXERCISE 5

Step 1: Role-Play and Feedback

- The client says the first beginner client statement. The counselor **improvises** a response based on the skill criteria.
- The trainer (or, if not available, the client) provides **brief** feedback based on the skill criteria.
- The client then repeats the same statement, and the counselor again improvises a response. The trainer (or client) again provides brief feedback.

Step 2: Repeat

- Repeat Step 1 for all the statements **in the current difficulty level** (beginner, intermediate, or advanced).

Step 3: Assess and Adjust Difficulty

- The counselor completes the Deliberate Practice Reaction Form (see Appendix A) and decides whether to make the exercise easier or harder or to repeat the same difficulty level.

Step 4: Repeat for Approximately 15 Minutes

- Repeat Steps 1 to 3 for at least 15 minutes.
- The trainees then switch counselor and client roles and start over.

> **Now it's your turn! Follow Steps 1 and 2 from the instructions.**

Remember: The goal of the role-play is for trainees to practice improvising responses to the client statements in a manner that (a) uses the skill criteria and (b) feels authentic for the trainee. **Example counselor responses for each client statement are provided at the end of this exercise. Trainees should attempt to improvise their own responses before reading the examples.**

BEGINNER-LEVEL CLIENT STATEMENTS FOR EXERCISE 5
Beginner Client Statement 1
[**Downtrodden**] I feel so unsatisfied and unfulfilled in my job. But I don't know that things could ever really get better.
Beginner Client Statement 2
[**Stressed**] I don't know how I'll ever decide which major is right for me. I'm in my second year of college, and I feel so much pressure to decide right away. It's overwhelming!
Beginner Client Statement 3
[**Discouraged**] I've been trying so hard in my pre-med major, but I just took the test exam for medical school, and my scores aren't very good. I've dreamed of being a doctor since I was a child. . . . Now what do I do?!
Beginner Client Statement 4
[**Depressed**] I'm widowed, and I don't have any family nearby. I'm considering retiring, but if I'm being really honest, I'm afraid I might get bored . . . or lonely. I'm all by myself as it is on the weekends. Maybe the weekdays would be lonely too if I stopped working. Anyways, I don't know why I'm even telling you this. How could you really help me? You only see me once every other week anyway.
Beginner Client Statement 5
[**Neutral**] My parents said I should come see you to work on myself. They think I should be more independent.

 Assess and adjust the difficulty before moving to the next difficulty level (see Step 3 in the exercise instructions).

INTERMEDIATE-LEVEL CLIENT STATEMENTS FOR EXERCISE 5
Intermediate Client Statement 1
[Nervous] I got a promotion at work. I know I should be excited about it, but I'm afraid I tricked people into thinking I'm actually smart enough for this job. I have this impending fear that I'm going to fail . . . big time. You probably think I should just be excited about getting a promotion, right? You're probably going to tell me I should just be grateful.
Intermediate Client Statement 2
[Irritated] Can't you just tell me what you think I should do about choosing a career? I mean, you're the expert here.
Intermediate Client Statement 3
[Anxious] It's been a pain coming to these sessions. My work schedule and the bus are both unpredictable, and I don't know if this is even worth it. How is this going to work?
Intermediate Client Statement 4
[Hopeless] I don't think I can do the informational interviews you suggested as homework. Honestly, I don't want to inconvenience anyone. And I don't know why you would even ask me to do that.
Intermediate Client Statement 5
[Frustrated] Why would you suggest I take career assessments? I'm already paying for our career counseling sessions, but you want me to pay another fee for these assessments on top of that? What good will they do me anyway?!

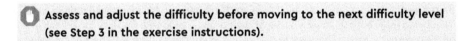 **Assess and adjust the difficulty before moving to the next difficulty level (see Step 3 in the exercise instructions).**

ADVANCED-LEVEL CLIENT STATEMENTS FOR EXERCISE 5
Advanced Client Statement 1
[Angry] My parents want me to go to college, but I'd rather get out and start making money at my friend's construction company. I'm tired of my parents telling me what to do! They even made me come here today! I don't know what the point of all of this "career counseling" stuff even is!
Advanced Client Statement 2
[Frustrated] I'm just not getting much out of our career counseling sessions. All we seem to do is talk about my interests. I already know what I'm interested in, but I don't know what to do about it!
Advanced Client Statement 3
[Annoyed] I'm struggling in my business major, and I'm worried about getting a job when I graduate, but why would I even go to business conferences this early in my studies? I know that's the homework we discussed that I do, but I'm too stressed with everything else.
Advanced Client Statement 4
[Melancholy] I'm so tired of trying at my job. I just feel like giving up. Everything feels too hard, and I'm ready to just call it quits.
Advanced Client Statement 5
[Nervous] I think I need to drop my classes for the semester. I'm behind on all my assignments and so stressed. My professors hate me, and at this point, I'm bound to fail.

 Assess and adjust the difficulty here (see Step 3 in the exercise instructions). If appropriate, follow the instructions to make the exercise even more challenging (see Appendix A).

Example Counselor Responses: Discussing the Benefits of Career Counseling

Remember: Trainees should attempt to improvise their own responses before reading the examples. **Do not read the following responses verbatim unless you are having trouble coming up with your own!**

EXAMPLE RESPONSES TO BEGINNER-LEVEL CLIENT STATEMENTS FOR EXERCISE 5
Example Response to Beginner Client Statement 1
I wonder if exploring your career values could be really useful. Once we narrow down your top values, we could explore careers that complement those values or things you could do outside of work to fulfill those values and help you find meaning. (Criteria 1 and 2) How would you feel about exploring your values, passions, dreams, and meaning? (Criterion 3)
Example Response to Beginner Client Statement 2
It sounds very stressful! One of the ways career counseling might help is by discussing your likes, dislikes, strengths, and what's most important to you and then exploring together careers and related majors that fit with those things. (Criteria 1 and 2) What are your thoughts about us starting there? (Criterion 3)
Example Response to Beginner Client Statement 3
I wonder if there may be some grief hidden in there? It can feel like a loss of our very identity when our hopes and dreams are shifted. Perhaps it could be helpful to explore your grief, in addition to considering alternative career paths that could complement a career in the medical field. (Criteria 1 and 2) Before we go much further, how would you feel about exploring your identity and the loss you might be feeling? (Criterion 3)
Example Response to Beginner Client Statement 4
I'm glad you did tell me this, because I think there are several things we could do in here that would help. To start, we can explore your thoughts and feelings about the transition, and we can talk about ways to help you connect with others, both in and outside of a vocation. (Criteria 1 and 2) How would you feel about exploring that together? (Criterion 3)
Example Response to Beginner Client Statement 5
I'd love to hear more about what being "independent" would mean to both you and your parents. We can also explore how you feel about having more autonomy and independence and can help you develop career plans that build on that. (Criteria 1 and 2) I wonder how you feel about talking through that together? (Criterion 3)

EXAMPLE RESPONSES TO INTERMEDIATE-LEVEL CLIENT STATEMENTS FOR EXERCISE 5

Example Response to Intermediate Client Statement 1

I hear the heaviness you've been carrying! I think our time together could be really useful if we explore those fears further, help you feel empowered in this new role, and develop a plan to set you up with support for success. (Criteria 1 and 2) What are your thoughts about us starting there? (Criterion 3)

Example Response to Intermediate Client Statement 2

I don't know the one "right" answer for you, but I do know that we can work on this together and figure it out. I know of a few career assessments, for example, that might help us explore some career options. (Criteria 1 and 2) Would you be open to trying that out as we start? (Criterion 3)

Example Response to Intermediate Client Statement 3

I definitely don't want career counseling to feel burdensome or like another thing you have to check off your already busy schedule. One thing we can do here is assess your interests and career concerns, and from there, we can see what goals you'd be interested in working on. (Criteria 1 and 2) Does that sound like something you'd be interested in? (Criterion 3)

Example Response to Intermediate Client Statement 4

I hear you and understand if that feels awkward. The reason I suggested informational interviews is because they can be a great way to learn more about potential career paths. We can also chat about other ways to explore career paths that you might prefer. (Criteria 1 and 2) Does the rationale for informational interviews make sense? . . . How would you feel about trying that out or, perhaps, exploring other ways of learning about career paths? (Criterion 3)

Example Response to Intermediate Client Statement 5

Career assessments can be useful to help you align your personal goals, interests, and strengths with particular careers. They can also help you evaluate skills you can use to market yourself during your job application and interview process. But if you don't feel comfortable taking those assessments, that's no problem—we can also talk through your interests, skills, and values one-on-one. (Criteria 1 and 2) What would you feel most comfortable with at this point? (Criterion 3)

EXAMPLE RESPONSES TO ADVANCED-LEVEL CLIENT STATEMENTS FOR EXERCISE 5

Example Response to Advanced Client Statement 1

I imagine you've been feeling really frustrated, and I can certainly understand feeling skeptical of this process. I wonder if it would feel helpful to brainstorm how you might talk with your parents about your interests and career goals. If you'd like, we could also explore careers related to construction or other things you enjoy. (Criteria 1 and 2) Would you be open to trying this out for a session or two to see if you're finding it helpful? (Criterion 3)

Example Response to Advanced Client Statement 2

I'm glad you let me know. Let's pivot a bit, then, and try something new. It sounds like focusing on an action plan would feel useful at this point. (Criteria 1 and 2) What are your thoughts about us developing some concrete plans for next steps in this session? (Criterion 3)

Example Response to Advanced Client Statement 3

It sounds like you've been really overwhelmed. Maybe it would be helpful if we slow this session down a bit, and I can explain why I suggested that particular homework assignment. One way career counseling can help is by supporting you in increasing your networking opportunities so that you get to know the ins and outs of your field and connect with potential future employers. Of course, we can find other ways to meet that goal besides going to business conferences. (Criteria 1 and 2) Would it feel useful to you if we spent some time brainstorming ways to network that don't involve attending conferences? (Criterion 3)

Example Response to Advanced Client Statement 4

I hear the heaviness in your heart, and I wonder if you're feeling burned out. Maybe it would be useful for us to spend some time today helping you develop some practical and attainable goals to develop more work–life balance. (Criteria 1 and 2) What feelings are coming up for you as we talk about work–life balance and work burnout? (Criterion 3)

Example Response to Advanced Client Statement 5

I can hear how overwhelmed you are as you speak. One way we can help here today is to spend some time talking through your options because I do think you have several options open to you. (Criteria 1 and 2) How would you feel about us focusing on developing a plan today? (Criterion 3)

EXERCISE 6

Setting Session Goals

Preparations for Exercise 6

1. Read the instructions in Chapter 2.
2. Download the Deliberate Practice Reaction Form and the Deliberate Practice Diary Form at https://www.apa.org/pubs/books/deliberate-practice-career-counseling (see the "Resources" tab; also available in Appendixes A and B, respectively).

Skill Description

Skill Difficulty Level: Intermediate

Determining the direction for each career counseling session is a critical skill in your career counseling toolbox. This exercise will help you gain skills to listen thoughtfully to what your client shares and work collaboratively toward goals that target your client's needs.

There are often many fruitful directions for career counseling clients. Each example response in this exercise represents just one of many potentially useful directions for a career counseling session. However, to be maximally effective, keep in mind the following guardrail: Any suggestion the career counselor offers for the direction of the career counseling session should be directly relevant to the specific concern or topic raised by the client. In other words, the suggestions must be client-centered rather than suggestions based on the counselor's general curiosity or interest.

To demonstrate this skill, the counselor should improvise a response to each client statement following these skill criteria:

1. **Acknowledge what the client shared with you.** Beginning by acknowledging what your client has shared with you can both validate and normalize what your client has disclosed and how they are feeling. Start with an empathic statement or summary of what they have shared.

---

https://doi.org/10.1037/0000442-008

Deliberate Practice in Career Counseling, by J. M. Taylor, A. Vaz, and T. Rousmaniere

Copyright © 2025 by the American Psychological Association. All rights reserved.

2. **Based on the client's statement, suggest a direction for the career counseling session.** In this second step, you will suggest a goal or direction for the career counseling session focused on responding to the challenges your client is currently facing. For example, some common directions include the following:

- Exploring your client's personal values and how they can more effectively honor and capitalize on those values in their current work activities or how those values may impact the meaning and satisfaction they derive from particular career(s) they are considering (see also Exercise 2).
- Assessing your client's current skill set to explore careers that align with their strengths and/or to explore areas that could be further developed to prepare for a career of interest (see also Exercise 1).
- Examining your client's self-efficacy and self-talk, particularly if they have experienced a recent setback (e.g., job loss, failed exam), and how the messages they give themselves may be affecting them.
- Delving into your client's past experiences with careers and how those experiences shape the way they look at careers or career prospects today.
- Asking your client open-ended questions to explore their experiences with their current career (e.g., what they like most and least about their current roles, work environment, responsibilities).
- Introducing your client to tools for self-compassion or stress management, as relevant to their specific career concerns.
- Helping your client find greater work–life balance by conducting an inventory to explore their current work roles or responsibilities and what a typical day looks like for them, or by providing space for the client to brainstorm work efficiencies or ways they could advocate for themself at work.
- Providing support and strategies for a client who is experiencing discrimination or harassment in the workplace.
- Determining your client's decision-making style and how it may impact the way they approach career counseling and career decision making in particular.
- Discussing the results of a career assessment and reactions the client has to feedback from the assessment (keep such discussions as basic as possible for the purposes of this exercise; Exercise 7 provides more in-depth practice opportunities for discussing assessment results).
- Exploring career options for a client who is returning to the workplace (e.g., parents returning to a workplace setting, employees transitioning from one job to another).
- Surveying your client's current support network and brainstorming ways they might add to their career support network (e.g., finding mentors that address certain areas of need for the client).
- Investigating the cultural and familial messages your client has received about careers and how those messages impact their current views related to careers (e.g., what careers are considered "prestigious," "acceptable," or "a disappointment" based on your client's cultural background, gender, socioeconomic status, sexual orientation, religion, or ability status; if you should "work to live" or "live to work"; see also Exercise 4).
- Conducting a mock job interview with your client to help them prepare for upcoming job interviews (e.g., helping your client advocate for themself and

prepare responses to their strengths and weaknesses, interest in a specific job position, past experiences that demonstrate translatable skills).

3. **Check in with the client to ensure they are comfortable with your proposed session direction.** This last step is critical in this process because it serves as the linchpin in ensuring congruence between your proposed direction for the career counseling session and your client's needs and goals for their career counseling experience. It is important to be aware of the power dynamics at play in career counseling sessions and to foster an environment where your client feels both comfortable and empowered to engage actively as a collaborative partner in shaping their career counseling journey. Some clients may hesitate to assert themselves by suggesting a different direction or by sharing concerns about the session's direction unless you prompt and invite this discussion. It is also important to remain attuned to your client's nonverbal cues, which can provide valuable insights into their interest in your proposed direction for the session.

SKILL CRITERIA FOR EXERCISE 6

1. Acknowledge what the client shared with you.
2. Based on the client's statement, suggest a direction for the career counseling session (examples of common directions are provided in the skill description).
3. Check in with the client to ensure they are comfortable with your proposed session direction.

Examples of Counselors Using Goal-Setting Skills

Example 1

CLIENT: [*despondent*] I really hate my job. I wish I didn't have to work there anymore.

COUNSELOR: Yes, I hear that you don't feel motivated in your current job. (Criterion 1) Perhaps we could talk about what, in particular, you don't like about your current job, and if your current job doesn't feel like a good fit, how we might help you explore some alternative career options, based on your interests, values, and skills. (Criterion 2) Would that be something you'd be interested in? (Criterion 3)

Example 2

CLIENT: [*frustrated*] I hate that people always ask me what I want to do with my life. I mean, I'm just a freshman in college—how am I supposed to know?!

COUNSELOR: Yes! There's so much loaded pressure with questions like that! I get that choosing a career path feels like an overwhelming decision right now. (Criterion 1) Let's start with some small steps. Perhaps we can begin by exploring what experiences you've had with careers already and what you liked, or didn't like, about them. (Criterion 2) How does that sound? (Criterion 3)

Example 3

CLIENT: [*regretful*] I feel like I've lost "it." I used to be passionate about what I do . . . now it feels meaningless.

COUNSELOR: It sounds like the purpose you found in your job used to be really clear, but your job either doesn't feel that meaningful anymore, or it doesn't align with your current values. (Criterion 1) Perhaps we can spend some time exploring your top values and can work together to think through how those values could align better with what you do within your job. (Criterion 2) How do you feel about us starting there? (Criterion 3)

INSTRUCTIONS FOR EXERCISE 6
Step 1: Role-Play and Feedback
• The client says the first beginner client statement. The counselor **improvises** a response based on the skill criteria. • The trainer (or, if not available, the client) provides **brief** feedback based on the skill criteria. • The client then repeats the same statement, and the counselor again improvises a response. The trainer (or client) again provides brief feedback.
Step 2: Repeat
• Repeat Step 1 for all the statements **in the current difficulty level** (beginner, intermediate, or advanced).
Step 3: Assess and Adjust Difficulty
• The counselor completes the Deliberate Practice Reaction Form (see Appendix A) and decides whether to make the exercise easier or harder or to repeat the same difficulty level.
Step 4: Repeat for Approximately 15 Minutes
• Repeat Steps 1 to 3 for at least 15 minutes. • The trainees then switch counselor and client roles and start over.

> **Now it's your turn! Follow Steps 1 and 2 from the instructions.**

Remember: The goal of the role-play is for trainees to practice improvising responses to the client statements in a manner that (a) uses the skill criteria and (b) feels authentic for the trainee. **Example counselor responses for each client statement are provided at the end of this exercise. Trainees should attempt to improvise their own responses before reading the examples.**

BEGINNER-LEVEL CLIENT STATEMENTS FOR EXERCISE 6
Beginner Client Statement 1
[Apathetic] I just don't see the point in this job anymore. Like, what am I really doing to help anyone?
Beginner Client Statement 2
[Bored] I retired a few years ago. I don't even know what to do with my time anymore.
Beginner Client Statement 3
[Tired] I live in a constant state of stress at work. I don't know how much longer I can deal with this.
Beginner Client Statement 4
[Exasperated] My parents keep pressuring me to pursue a degree in mechanical engineering, but I'm failing all my math classes. I don't think I'm cut out for this.
Beginner Client Statement 5
[Hopeless] I've been out of work for nearly a year now. At this point, I don't even know what I'm good at anymore.

 Assess and adjust the difficulty before moving to the next difficulty level (see Step 3 in the exercise instructions).

INTERMEDIATE-LEVEL CLIENT STATEMENTS FOR EXERCISE 6
Intermediate Client Statement 1
[Inferior] Growing up, I saw my parents work and work and work. I've been trying to do the same for the last decade. I'm just so . . . tired.
Intermediate Client Statement 2
[Frustrated] I come home from work exhausted every day. From the moment I wake up, I'm working. Even at night when I sleep, I dream about my job and all the things I have to do!
Intermediate Client Statement 3
[Despondent] I feel so abandoned in my current job. My boss transitioned my position, and now I work remote. I rarely see my coworkers anymore.
Intermediate Client Statement 4
[Confused] I don't even know what I want out of my job anymore. All I know is that I'm so bored.
Intermediate Client Statement 5
[Discouraged] I don't even know who I'd turn to for help. I feel so alone at work.

 Assess and adjust the difficulty before moving to the next difficulty level (see Step 3 in the exercise instructions).

ADVANCED-LEVEL CLIENT STATEMENTS FOR EXERCISE 6

Advanced Client Statement 1

[Hurt] My boss made a sexist comment yesterday. I am so furious, I don't even know what to do!

Advanced Client Statement 2

[Frustrated] I think I made the wrong decision accepting this job. Now what do I do?!

Advanced Client Statement 3

[Ashamed] I don't even know how I got this job. I feel like a total imposter—like I tricked everyone into thinking I am actually good enough for this role. I just don't measure up.

Advanced Client Statement 4

[Stressed] I just lost my job, and I have three children I need to take care of at home. What am I going to do?!

Advanced Client Statement 5

[Skeptical] I don't even know if this whole "career counseling" thing is for me. I still don't have a job. How do I know if this is even working?

> ✋ Assess and adjust the difficulty here (see Step 3 in the exercise instructions). If appropriate, follow the instructions to make the exercise even more challenging (see Appendix A).

Example Counselor Responses: Goal Setting

Remember: Trainees should attempt to improvise their own responses before reading the examples. **Do not read the following responses verbatim unless you are having trouble coming up with your own!**

EXAMPLE RESPONSES TO BEGINNER-LEVEL CLIENT STATEMENTS FOR EXERCISE 6
Example Response to Beginner Client Statement 1
It sounds like you're struggling to find meaning in your current job. (Criterion 1) Let's spend some time looking at what a "meaningful" job would mean to you. We can explore your purpose and where that purpose currently aligns or could align better either in your current job or another one. (Criterion 2) How does that sound to you? (Criterion 3)
Example Response to Beginner Client Statement 2
Now there's almost too much free time! (Criterion 1) Let's delve in a bit more and explore what you're passionate about. (Criterion 2) How would you feel about us exploring that further? (Criterion 3)
Example Response to Beginner Client Statement 3
I hear how overwhelmed you've felt. (Criterion 1) I wonder what it would feel like if we paused for a moment and looked at ways to sneak in some moments of self-care throughout the day. We can explore what self-care means to you and strategize ways to help you fit moments of self-care in. (Criterion 2) Would that be okay with you? (Criterion 3)
Example Response to Beginner Client Statement 4
This sounds like it's been really stressful! Your parents are encouraging you to pursue a degree that doesn't seem to align with your current skills and knowledge, and it's making you question if this is the right major for you. (Criterion 1) I wonder what it would feel like to start by taking a step back and exploring where you see your strengths. (Criterion 2) How would you feel about us starting there? (Criterion 3)
Example Response to Beginner Client Statement 5
I hear how discouraged you've felt. It's even made you question your skills in a new job. (Criterion 1) We could address this question by exploring your strengths and the skills you bring to a new job. (Criterion 2) Would you feel comfortable with us starting by exploring this further? (Criterion 3)

EXAMPLE RESPONSES TO INTERMEDIATE-LEVEL CLIENT STATEMENTS FOR EXERCISE 6

Example Response to Intermediate Client Statement 1

It sounds exhausting. (Criterion 1) Let's talk about the hustle you've been under. How would slowing down shift your daily life? In what ways do you feel that slowing down would help or hurt you? (Criterion 2) Would you be okay with us jumping in and discussing this further? (Criterion 3)

Example Response to Intermediate Client Statement 2

I hear the exhaustion in your voice, and I hear the struggle to find any sort of work–life balance. (Criterion 1) Sometimes it can be really difficult to turn work "off." Let's pause for a moment and look at what "being busy" means to you. We can explore what it would feel like to slow down and what that would mean to you. (Criterion 2) How do you feel about starting there? (Criterion 3)

Example Response to Intermediate Client Statement 3

It sounds like work has felt really isolating. (Criterion 1) Perhaps we can start by exploring ways to help you connect more with others, either in your current job or in your time outside of work. (Criterion 2) How would you feel about us starting there? (Criterion 3)

Example Response to Intermediate Client Statement 4

I understand. It's been really discouraging. It's hard to work at a place that doesn't feel meaningful. (Criterion 1) I wonder if there are ways we could capitalize more on your values at work. We could start by trying out a values card sort to explore what values are most important to you in your career and then brainstorm together some ways you might be able to more intentionally infuse those values in your current job or in your life outside of work? (Criterion 2) How would you feel about us beginning there? (Criterion 3)

Example Response to Intermediate Client Statement 5

I hear that work has felt really isolating. (Criterion 1) Because you're not sure who to turn to for help at work, why don't we spend a bit of time today looking at your mentors—either ones you can currently call on or ways to find and advocate for a community network of mentors? (Criterion 2) Would you be open to us creating a plan to deepen and widen your mentoring network? (Criterion 3)

EXAMPLE RESPONSES TO ADVANCED-LEVEL CLIENT STATEMENTS FOR EXERCISE 6

Example Response to Advanced Client Statement 1

I feel angry just hearing about that! (Criterion 1) It feels so disempowering to hear people in positions of power degrading others, including ourselves. Perhaps we can spend some time today brainstorming ways to take your power back. But before we get there, I'd like to hear more about the conversation and any concerns you might hold about repercussions or barriers to addressing this. (Criterion 2) How would you feel about us starting there? (Criterion 3)

Example Response to Advanced Client Statement 2

It sounds like you're feeling a sense of regret with this job. (Criterion 1) Let's explore your expectations for the job a bit more and where the job aligns and doesn't with what you expected. (Criterion 2) How would you feel about us starting there? (Criterion 3)

Example Response to Advanced Client Statement 3

Ouch! I hear a lot of pain and fears embedded in what you're sharing. (Criterion 1) Maybe we could spend some time today focusing on this fear that you are an imposter; we can work to identify where that stemmed from, explore the messages you've received, and work to deconstruct those messages and infuse some self-compassion. (Criterion 2) How would you feel about that? (Criterion 3)

Example Response to Advanced Client Statement 4

You're dealing with so much right now. I hear the heaviness and stress you are facing. (Criterion 1) So let's start by making sure your basic needs are met and, if not, coming up with a plan together to get you and your family resources. Then we can delve into next steps for finding new employment and managing the stress you're currently under. (Criterion 2) How does that sound? (Criterion 3)

Example Response to Advanced Client Statement 5

I hear you, and I also understand how frustrating it's been to be out of work. (Criterion 1) Let's talk through a plan together to ensure you're getting the most out of our sessions together. What do you hope and expect in our sessions? (Criterion 2) Would that work for you as a starting point? (Criterion 3)

Exercise 7

Feedback on Career Assessments

Preparations for Exercise 7

1. Read the instructions in Chapter 2.
2. Download the Deliberate Practice Reaction Form and the Deliberate Practice Diary Form at https://www.apa.org/pubs/books/deliberate-practice-career-counseling (see the "Resources" tab; also available in Appendixes A and B, respectively).

Skill Description

Skill Difficulty Level: Advanced

A range of assessments can be used in career counseling: assessments of values, personality, skills, and interests, to name a few. However, the actions career counselors take after administering career assessments are often more of an art than a science. This exercise is designed to help career counselors as they craft the career counseling session that follows the assessments. If self-understanding is the artwork and the goal, a career counselor's ability to reflect on the client's assessment report is the paintbrush, and thoughtful questions and comments are the paint.

In a real career counseling session, it can be useful to ask about the client's experience while taking the assessment. What was their reaction to taking it? Did the answers come easily or was it difficult? Did they have any questions along the way? Were there any life conditions at the time they took the assessment that may have influenced their responses? Career assessments can provide useful information, but processing the client's experience can help dramatically in contextualizing the results.

This deliberate practice exercise is slightly different from the other ones in this book. Instead of having a participant read client statements as prompts for skills practice, they will read scripted "context prompts," providing information on the results of a career assessment. The next exercise, which follows the same format with similar client

---

https://doi.org/10.1037/0000442-009

Deliberate Practice in Career Counseling, by J. M. Taylor, A. Vaz, and T. Rousmaniere

Copyright © 2025 by the American Psychological Association. All rights reserved.

contexts, builds on the skills in this exercise by asking trainees to explore the underlying themes of clients' assessment results.

The counselor should improvise a response to each context prompt following these skill criteria:

1. **Reflect the major observations(s) the assessment might be indicating for the client.** This first step is useful to frame the feedback session. In this step, the career counselor highlights a key observation from the assessment results. It can be helpful to choose an observation that directly relates to the client's primary reason for taking the career assessment. For example, if a client is deciding between two college majors, it may be worthwhile to explore a specific value or interest that appears, based on assessment results, and to highlight that value or interest as it relates to each potential major.

2. **Convey that any suggestions for specific work areas are only suggestions, and what matters is the fit with the client.** Some career assessments can feel prescriptive, and it is important to treat conversations about career assessments as an opportunity for a discussion with your client rather than an "order." Some career assessments, for example, provide specific suggested career paths for clients. Clients may experience one of three reactions to those career suggestions: (a) relief and confirmation for career paths they were already considering, (b) frustration that the career paths suggested do not seem to fit with their perceived options and interests, or (c) a deferential attitude or resignation that those must be the "right" paths for the client. Rather than presenting proposed career paths as a prescription for the "correct" career, frame the proposed careers as some fields that might interest the client, align with some of their values, or spark related career paths that may also be worth considering. On the surface, some career paths may be of little interest to a client, but if the career counselor asks more about the client's inherent interests or values, some interests or values present in that career path may highlight a client's salient interest or value. For example, a client may be surprised to see "judge" listed as a potential career option for them. While the career path of a judge may not be a good fit, careers that embody the spirit of justice as a value may be worth further career exploration.

3. **Invite the client to elaborate on their thoughts and reactions around these test results.** This last step is critical and involves creating a conversation with the client. It is exceptionally useful to provide space for clients to share their thoughts and feelings about the assessment results. It is important that career counselors ask open-ended questions and invite their clients to share openly any reactions, surprises, relief, or even disagreements they might have with the career assessment feedback.

SKILL CRITERIA FOR EXERCISE 7

1. Reflect the major observations(s) the assessment might be indicating for the client.
2. Convey that any suggestions for specific work areas are only suggestions, and what matters is the fit with the client.
3. Invite the client to elaborate on their thoughts and reactions around these test results.

Examples of Counselors Providing Feedback on Career Assessments

Example 1

CONTEXT: The client's assessment results suggest that they enjoy working with others and working in settings where they make clear social contributions. An example of a potential career path provided by the assessment is working in a hospital as a medical doctor or nurse.

COUNSELOR: I reviewed your career assessment results, and the results suggest that you may be interested in working with others and making meaningful contributions to your community. Some examples of potential career paths this assessment suggests are working as a medical doctor or nurse. (Criterion 1) Even though this assessment suggests you might be interested in working as a doctor or nurse, those particular professions might not interest you. What matters right now is exploring the values and interests underlying these job suggestions. (Criterion 2) So I'd love to hear from you: What are your thoughts about these suggestions? Do these results seem to align, or not, with your areas of interest? (Criterion 3)

Example 2

CONTEXT: The client's assessment results suggest that they crave stability in their careers. An example of a career path that may be of interest to this client is real estate appraisal.

COUNSELOR: I'm excited to explore the results of your career assessment with you today! One interesting result I noticed was that you seem to value stability in your career path and may be interested in careers that reflect stability, such as real estate appraising. (Criterion 1) I do want to note that while the results of the assessment suggest specific careers, real estate appraising itself may or may not be of interest to you. What's most important is exploring specific careers that fit with your own interests and values. (Criterion 2) I'm curious to hear more about your reactions to the results of the assessment. Is finding a stable career is an important—even top—consideration for you in relation to exploring career options? (Criterion 3)

Example 3

CONTEXT: The client's assessment results suggest that they are skilled at teaching. Two career paths suggested through the assessment are a career as a professor or a motivational speaker.

COUNSELOR: Let's dive in to explore the results of the skill assessment you took last week! The results suggest you might be especially skilled at teaching and might be interested in a career path in a field that capitalizes on your teaching skills, such as working as a professor or a motivational speaker. (Criterion 1) Keep in mind that the specific career paths listed in the assessment results represent suggestions of career paths that may be a good fit rather than directions for a specific career path you "should" choose. We'll focus today on exploring careers that interest you and align with your top skills. (Criterion 2) As we begin to go through your assessment results, let's pause for a minute: What are your reactions to hearing that teaching may be a top skill for you? (Criterion 3)

INSTRUCTIONS FOR EXERCISE 7

Step 1: Role-Play and Feedback

- The client says the first beginner context prompt. The counselor **improvises** a response based on the skill criteria.
- The trainer (or, if not available, the client) provides **brief** feedback based on the skill criteria.
- The client then repeats the same context prompt, and the counselor again improvises a response. The trainer (or client) again provides brief feedback.

Step 2: Repeat

- Repeat Step 1 for all the statements **in the current difficulty level** (beginner, intermediate, or advanced).

Step 3: Assess and Adjust Difficulty

- The counselor completes the Deliberate Practice Reaction Form (see Appendix A) and decides whether to make the exercise easier or harder or to repeat the same difficulty level.

Step 4: Repeat for Approximately 15 Minutes

- Repeat Steps 1 to 3 for at least 15 minutes.
- The trainees then switch counselor and client roles and start over.

Now it's your turn! Follow Steps 1 and 2 from the instructions.

Remember: The goal of the role-play is for trainees to practice improvising responses to the client contexts in a manner that (a) uses the skill criteria and (b) feels authentic for the trainee. **Example counselor responses for each client context are provided at the end of this exercise. Trainees should attempt to improvise their own responses before reading the examples.**

BEGINNER-LEVEL CLIENT CONTEXTS FOR EXERCISE 7
Beginner Client Context 1
The client decided to engage in career counseling because they are unhappy in their current job. The client's assessment results suggest that they value opportunities for advancement at work. One suggested career path is a sales force developer.
Beginner Client Context 2
The client decided to engage in career counseling because they want to decide on a college major within the next month. Their skill assessment results suggest that they are self-motivated. Results suggest that career paths of interest may be a chef, salesperson, social media coordinator, or investment banker.
Beginner Client Context 3
The client decided to engage in career counseling because they are interviewing with three potential employers and are undecided as to which organization may be the best fit for them. Results from a values assessment suggest that they value work–life balance in their career. The results suggest career paths of interest might include a copy editor or a freelance writer.
Beginner Client Context 4
The client decided to pursue career counseling because they are not happy in their current major, and they would like to explore other potential areas of study. Results from a personality assessment suggest that they are open-minded and imaginative. A few potential career paths that capitalize on creativity include journalism, interior design, advertising, marketing, architecture, and web development.
Beginner Client Context 5
The client decided to pursue career counseling because they were recently laid off at work, and they are now considering a career transition. Results from a personality assessment suggest that they are assertive and energetic. Careers that align with this personality type might include lawyer, sales manager, and event planner.

 Assess and adjust the difficulty before moving to the next difficulty level (see Step 3 in the exercise instructions).

INTERMEDIATE-LEVEL CLIENT CONTEXTS FOR EXERCISE 7
Intermediate Client Context 1
The client decided to pursue career counseling because they are graduating from high school in a few months and would like to consider a range of career options. Results from a values card sort suggest that they value working independently. Some related career paths include photographer, web designer, economist, actuary, graphic designer, and accountant.
Intermediate Client Context 2
The client decided to pursue career counseling because they want to engage in greater self-awareness and pursue a career path that aligns with their values. Results from a values assessment suggest that they strongly value creativity. A few relevant career paths might include graphic designer, game designer, and event management.
Intermediate Client Context 3
The client decided to pursue career counseling because they feel unchallenged in their current work environment and would like to consider alternative career paths. Results from a skills assessment suggest that possess attention to detail. Some related careers include computer programmer, quality assurance and compliance, editor, customer service representative, and data analyst.
Intermediate Client Context 4
The client decided to pursue career counseling because they are feeling pressure from their parents to pursue a degree in medicine, but they are failing their pre-med courses. Results from a skills assessment suggest they excel at persuading others. A few related careers include sales manager, lawyer, architectural manager, or judge.
Intermediate Client Context 5
The client decided to pursue career counseling because their current job feels stagnant, and they would like to consider alternative career paths. Results from a values assessment suggest that they value challenges at work and possess good critical thinking skills. A few proposed career paths for critical thinkers like this client are air traffic controller, computer scientist, and social worker.

 Assess and adjust the difficulty before moving to the next difficulty level (see Step 3 in the exercise instructions).

ADVANCED-LEVEL CLIENT CONTEXTS FOR EXERCISE 7

Advanced Client Context 1

The client decided to engage in career counseling because they are unhappy in their current major, media and journalism. Results from a skills assessment suggest that they are skilled at writing and other creative endeavors, and one suggested career path is journalist.

Advanced Client Context 2

The client decided to engage in career counseling because they are graduating soon and are wondering what questions they should ask at job interviews to assess fit between their skill set and the company's needs. Results from a skills assessment suggest that they excel at working in teams. Some related careers include human resources manager, consultant, market researcher, and product assembler.

Advanced Client Context 3

The client decided to engage in career counseling because they are pursuing a master's degree in clinical mental health counseling but are unsure what career path they would like to pursue with this degree. Their values assessment results suggest that a key value for them is social justice. The assessment results suggest that the client may be interested in pursuing a career as a clinical mental health counselor.

Advanced Client Context 4

The client decided to engage in career counseling because they are feeling pressure to pursue a degree in law from their parents, but the client does not believe they are competent to pursue this path. They feel generally worn down and tired. A values assessment suggests that they would enjoy a stable, low-risk work environment. A few relatively stable careers include respiratory therapist, financial analyst, school psychologist, and landscaper.

Advanced Client Context 5

The client decided to pursue career counseling because they are trying to decide between two college majors: statistics and psychology. Results from a skills assessment suggest that they may excel in programming, but the client has explicitly stated that they do not want to follow their parents' career path, which, ironically, is computer programming.

 Assess and adjust the difficulty here (see Step 3 in the exercise instructions). If appropriate, follow the instructions to make the exercise even more challenging (see Appendix A).

Example Counselor Responses: Feedback on Career Assessments

Remember: Trainees should attempt to improvise their own responses before reading the examples. **Do not read the following responses verbatim unless you are having trouble coming up with your own!**

EXAMPLE RESPONSES TO BEGINNER-LEVEL CLIENT CONTEXTS FOR EXERCISE 7

Example Response to Beginner Client Context 1

The results from this values assessment suggest you would thrive in careers that allow you the opportunity for advancement and promotion. While this specific measure also suggests career paths that may align with your values, like a sales force developer, (Criterion 1) keep in mind that the proposed careers represent only a portion of those that may interest you, and what matters most is the alignment between what you view as your top values and particular careers. (Criterion 2) As you look at these results, I'd love to hear more about your thoughts and reactions: Do they seem to align with important work values you hold? Are there areas in which those proposed values seem misaligned? (Criterion 3)

Example Response to Beginner Client Context 2

This aptitude assessment suggests you are self-motivated and would excel in careers that capitalize on and support your driven nature. A few potential career paths to get us started thinking about career options could be careers as a chef, salesperson, social media coordinator, or investment banker. (Criterion 1) You might notice that the career paths I mentioned are quite broad and expansive. These career paths are only a few suggestions that may be of interest to you. As we look at these results together, let's keep in mind your top interests, values, and skills and how they may or may not align with the careers the assessment report offers or others you may be considering as you think about your college major. (Criterion 2) As we begin, let's pause for a moment; how important would it feel to you to find a career that supports your driven nature and that provides autonomy for self-motivation? (Criterion 3)

Example Response to Beginner Client Context 3

Your test results suggest you value work–life balance and careers that allow for flexibility. Some specific careers that reflect this work–life balance include copy editor or freelance writer. (Criterion 1) It is important to note, however, that these careers only represent a few examples of careers that offer work–life balance flexibility that may be appealing to you. (Criterion 2) As you think about your upcoming job interviews and the results of this values assessment, I'm curious if work–life balance might be one aspect you'd want to learn more about with each prospective employer? (Criterion 3)

Example Response to Beginner Client Context 4

Results from this particular assessment suggest you are creative and open-minded and may enjoy careers that allow your imagination to thrive. A few potential majors might include journalism, interior design, advertising, marketing, architecture, or web development. (Criterion 1) Let's keep in mind, though, that these are just a few majors that may be of interest to you. What's most important is for us to take some time together to think through a range of majors to see if they align well with your personality. (Criterion 2) How well do the descriptions of imagination and open-mindedness seem to align with your view of yourself? What are your reactions to hearing this about yourself? (Criterion 3)

EXAMPLE RESPONSES TO BEGINNER-LEVEL CLIENT CONTEXTS FOR EXERCISE 7

Example Response to Beginner Client Context 5

These assessment results suggest you are an assertive and energetic person who may thrive in work conditions that value positive energy and reward assertiveness. Some related careers include, but of course are not limited to, law, sales, and event planning. (Criterion 1) It's important to note, however, that these career paths represent only a small portion of those that may align with your personality traits, so let's spend some time exploring potential career options that align with your personality and interests. (Criterion 2) How well does that description seem to describe you and careers you've been in previously? (Criterion 3)

EXAMPLE RESPONSES TO INTERMEDIATE-LEVEL CLIENT CONTEXTS FOR EXERCISE 7

Example Response to Intermediate Client Context 1

The results from your values assessment suggest that you would enjoy working in an environment that allows for autonomy and independence. A few related career paths include photographer, web designer, economist, actuary, graphic designer, and accountant. (Criterion 1) Keep in mind that these are only a few careers that may align with your values. Importantly, today we'll spend some time exploring a range of careers that align with your values and interests. (Criterion 2) I'm curious to hear your reactions to the values assessment and whether careers that involve independent work would feel like a good fit for you. What are your reactions? (Criterion 3)

Example Response to Intermediate Client Context 2

The values assessment suggests that you value creativity highly and may enjoy a career that prioritizes it. A few related careers include graphic designer, game designer, and event management. (Criterion 1) Keep in mind, however, that these careers only represent a few of those that capitalize on creativity. While those specific career paths may not be of interest to you, we'll spend some time today looking at a range of careers that, importantly, align with your interests and values. (Criterion 2) While we're on that note, I'd love to hear your thoughts and reactions—both related to the careers I mentioned and whether creativity feels like an important value you'd like to cultivate in your career path. (Criterion 3)

Example Response to Intermediate Client Context 3

Let's take a look together at your aptitude assessment. This assessment suggests that you shine in relation to attention to detail and may do well in a career that capitalizes on that. A few careers that depend on conscientious employees include computer programmer, quality assurance and compliance, editor, customer service representative, and data analyst. (Criterion 1) Keep in mind that these careers represent only a few that may align with your skill set. We'll take some time next to explore careers that align with your specific skills and your interests and values as well. (Criterion 2) Before we delve in much further, let's pause for a moment. What are your thoughts and reactions to hearing about these test results? In what ways do they align, or not, with your view of your strengths? (Criterion 3)

Example Response to Intermediate Client Context 4

Let's take a moment to look at your aptitude test results. One interesting thing I found in your results is that you seem to have a particular skill in influencing others. There are many careers that may align well with someone skilled at persuasion. A few include sales manager, lawyer, architectural manager, or judge. (Criterion 1) Keep in mind, though, that these are just a few of many careers that may be of interest to you. What we'll focus on today is looking at career paths that align with your top skills, interests, values, and personality. (Criterion 2) As I mentioned, the career assessment suggests that you are skilled in influencing others. I'm curious to hear your thoughts on this: Would you have any interest in careers that align with the skill of persuasion? Why or why not? (Criterion 3)

> **EXAMPLE RESPONSES TO INTERMEDIATE-LEVEL CLIENT CONTEXTS FOR EXERCISE 7**
>
> *Example Response to Intermediate Client Context 5*
>
> Your test results seem to explain why you may have felt frustrated in your last job; the results suggest that you enjoy work settings that challenge you, involve critical thinking, and offer opportunities for growth. A few careers that may align with this value include air traffic controller, computer scientist, and social worker. (Criterion 1) But remember, these careers are only a few of many that may be of interest to you. Today we'll look at a range of careers that align with your interests, values, skills, and personality. (Criterion 2) Before we explore specific careers, let's pause for a moment. I mentioned that the test suggests you like a good challenge at work. I'm curious if that assessment seemed to fit you? (Criterion 3)

EXAMPLE RESPONSES TO ADVANCED-LEVEL CLIENT CONTEXTS FOR EXERCISE 7

Example Response to Advanced Client Context 1

Your career assessment results suggest that you have a particular talent in writing and may enjoy a career that uses creativity and self-expression. Interestingly, your results also suggest you might enjoy a career as a journalist, an area I know you've been unhappy in. (Criterion 1) It's important to note that the career paths suggested in this report represent just a handful of careers that focus on the skills of creativity and self-expression. What we'll focus on today is exploring a range of career paths that highlight the skills of self-expression, creativity, research, planning and outlining, and editing—all skills that underlie the overarching skill of writing. (Criterion 2) Before we explore any specific careers, though, let's pause. I'm curious to hear your reaction to these results. When you think about careers that you would find interesting, how important, or not, is it to you to utilize your skills in self-expression and writing? (Criterion 3)

Example Response to Advanced Client Context 2

I'm excited to chat with you about your assessment report! One interesting thing I found when I read through it was that you are likely very skilled at working with others and could thrive in work environments that utilize team-based models. (Criterion 1) Keep in mind, though, that the results of this assessment are simply suggestions. What matters most is what you think about these results and how they do, or don't, align with your own interests and skills. (Criterion 2) Let's take a moment to look at the results further: The test seems to suggest you would excel working in teams. I'm curious to hear your thoughts about that. What has your experience been like in the past when you've worked in teams? (Criterion 3)

Example Response to Advanced Client Context 3

While the careers assessment results are broad and suggest that you might be interested in a career as a counselor, one particularly interesting thing I found when I was looking at your assessment results was that social justice may be a strong value of yours. (Criterion 1) It's important to keep in perspective that although we'll talk about a lot of assessment results and potential career paths today, what I'd like for us to focus on is the fit between your values and a range of career paths. (Criterion 2) So as we jump into this, let's start by focusing on social justice. I'd love to hear if that feels like it fits, or not, as an important value you hold in your life. How has it shown up, or not, in your careers, hobbies, or volunteering? (Criterion 3)

Example Response to Advanced Client Context 4

I'm looking forward to discussing the results of your values assessment; there's a lot for us to explore together! Of note, your results suggest that you value stable, low-risk work environments, which might explain why you've felt some hesitation and pause with relatively high-pressure careers. A few career paths that tend to be stable include respiratory therapist, financial analyst, school psychologist, and landscaper. (Criterion 1) These careers are only a few of many that may fit with your values, so we'll spend some time today both exploring and also narrowing down career paths that align with your values. (Criterion 2) To begin, I'm curious to hear whether low-risk, stable work environments are important to you and how this aligns, or doesn't, with careers you might pursue in law. (Criterion 3)

> **EXAMPLE RESPONSES TO ADVANCED-LEVEL CLIENT CONTEXTS FOR EXERCISE 7**
>
> *Example Response to Advanced Client Context 5*
>
> Thanks for taking the time to complete the skills assessment! There are many rich assessment results I'd like to chat with you about today. Interestingly, the assessment suggests you would be successful in careers related to programming, although I recognize you've mentioned that you are not interested in pursuing your parents' career path. (Criterion 1) What we'll keep in mind as we go through the results together is how well, or not, your skills align with a range of majors, recognizing, too, that the majors suggestions included in this specific assessment represent just a few of many majors that may be of interest to and in alignment with you. (Criterion 2) While pursuing a degree in programming may not be of interest to you, I wonder if there are skills and interests that underlie that major that would be. Let's take a moment to explore that further . . . what is it about programming that you like the least, and what do you like the most? (Criterion 3)

Exploring Underlying Themes in Assessments

Preparations for Exercise 8

1. Read the instructions in Chapter 2.

2. Download the Deliberate Practice Reaction Form and the Deliberate Practice Diary Form at https://www.apa.org/pubs/books/deliberate-practice-career-counseling (see the "Resources" tab; also available in Appendixes A and B, respectively).

Skill Description

Skill Difficulty Level: Advanced

This exercise is a continuation of the previous one (Exercise 7, "Feedback on Career Assessments"), focusing on the more advanced skill of exploring underlying themes in assessment results. Assessment results provide many details about a client; they may provide insights about their skills, their interests, or their values. While any client can read the assessment results, the true skills of a career counselor come into play when exploring the result's underlying themes—how the assessment results hang together.

Note that naming the underlying theme accurately matters much less than does facilitating a fruitful conversation about the results themselves. The goal here is to help the client explore and uncover their interests, values, and skills, not necessarily to guess the right answer. Focus on what you are curious about and look at the overall gestalt of your client's responses—what patterns do you notice? What skills, interests, or values seem to keep repeating or stand out across assessments?

It is also important to note that although some career assessments include suggestions for specific career paths that may be appealing to a client, a client may not be interested in that specific career path. In situations like this, the skill of uncovering underlying themes in assessment results becomes particularly important. For example, an assessment result might suggest a client is interested in being a police officer when, in fact, that is not a specific career path that they are interested in pursuing. However, the underlying theme

https://doi.org/10.1037/0000442-010
Deliberate Practice in Career Counseling, by J. M. Taylor, A. Vaz, and T. Rousmaniere
Copyright © 2025 by the American Psychological Association. All rights reserved.

may suggest that they are interested in justice, order, and accountability, and it may be useful to consider with the client careers that connect with those value themes.

Keeping this in mind, the counselor should improvise a response to each client context or situation following these skill criteria:

1. **Convey that any suggestions for specific work areas are only suggestions and what matters is the fit with the client.** Although many assessment results may suggest specific career paths, it is rarely helpful to use assessments as prescriptions for a specific career a client should pursue; rather, consider using assessments to facilitate a larger conversation around the client's interests, skills, and/or values, as noted in themes that arose from the assessment(s). This initial disclaimer, that any specific career suggestions are merely suggestions, is helpful to note because it gives the client permission to share honestly their reactions to a range of career paths proposed. In real clinical practice, you should gauge your client's reactions to proposed careers as you discuss them and make a mental note of those reactions. It may be valuable to explore those reactions further as the session progresses. For now, however, the main purpose of this step is to provide a disclaimer that while the assessment report may name specific careers that may be of interest to the client, what matters most is the client's own interest in a particular career.

2. **Suggest a larger underlying theme that might align with this client based on the suggestions provided by the assessment.** This criterion is really the heart—and main challenge—of this exercise. In this second step, suggest a theme that might undergird the client's assessment results. The goal in this step is not necessarily to pinpoint the theme accurately but rather to facilitate a conversation around potential themes, so make sure to state the observed theme as a suggestion; invite curiosity surrounding the potential theme. This leads to the last step: Check in with your client.

3. **Invite the client to reflect on the potential underlying theme.** In this final step, you will ask the client a question to help them dig deeper into the proposed theme. Consider, for example, asking an open-ended question that builds from the theme you have noticed, or ask the client how that theme connects with their past work experiences; alternatively, you might ask how that theme connects with their cultural or familial values (see Exercise 4).

SKILL CRITERIA FOR EXERCISE 8

1. Convey that any suggestions for specific work areas are only suggestions and what matters is the fit with the client.
2. Suggest a larger underlying theme that might align with this client based on the suggestions provided by the assessment.
3. Invite the client to reflect on the potential underlying theme.

Examples of Career Counselors Exploring Underlying Themes in Assessments

Example 1

CONTEXT: The client's assessment results suggest an example of a potential career path for this client could be working in a hospital as a medical doctor or nurse. The client has explicitly said they are not interested in these particular jobs.

COUNSELOR: You've mentioned that you are not particularly interested in working in a hospital, so let's focus instead on brainstorming career options that fit your values and interests. (Criterion 1) I wonder if this assessment might be picking up on a larger theme of you potentially enjoying working with others and working in settings where you would make clear societal contributions. (Criterion 2) As you think about your interests and values, how important is it to you that the career path involves helping others and making societal contributions? (Criterion 3)

Example 2

CONTEXT: The client's interest assessment results suggest a few career paths that may be of interest to this client are real estate appraiser, school psychologist, and epidemiologist, which are considered relatively secure career paths.

COUNSELOR: A few careers highlighted as suggestions in your assessment report include a real estate appraiser, school psychologist, and epidemiologist, but keep in mind that these are just a few of many career paths that may be of interest to you. What we'll concentrate on today are careers that fit with your interests and values. (Criterion 1) I wonder if these career paths may be pointing us to an underlying theme related to an interest in stable, secure jobs. (Criterion 2) What are your thoughts? (Criterion 3)

Example 3

CONTEXT: Two career paths suggested through the client's assessment report are a career as a professor or a motivational speaker.

COUNSELOR: The results of your assessment suggest a career as a professor or motivational speaker may be a good fit. However, let's dig in a bit deeper, because there may be a theme that connects those career paths, and there may even be other careers that you might be interested in. (Criterion 1) I wonder if a connecting theme for you might center on your interest in teaching, training, or inspiring others? (Criterion 2) As you think about your ideal career—one that invigorates you—to what degree do those careers involve educating, mentoring, and inspiring others? (Criterion 3)

INSTRUCTIONS FOR EXERCISE 8

Step 1: Role-Play and Feedback

- The client says the first beginner context prompt. The counselor **improvises** a response based on the skill criteria.
- The trainer (or, if not available, the client) provides **brief** feedback based on the skill criteria.
- The client then repeats the same context prompt, and the counselor again improvises a response. The trainer (or client) again provides brief feedback.

Step 2: Repeat

- Repeat Step 1 for all the statements **in the current difficulty level** (beginner, intermediate, or advanced).

Step 3: Assess and Adjust Difficulty

- The counselor completes the Deliberate Practice Reaction Form (see Appendix A) and decides whether to make the exercise easier or harder or to repeat the same difficulty level.

Step 4: Repeat for Approximately 15 Minutes

- Repeat Steps 1 to 3 for at least 15 minutes.
- The trainees then switch counselor and client roles and start over.

Now it's your turn! Follow Steps 1 and 2 from the instructions.

Remember: The goal of the role-play is for trainees to practice improvising responses to the client context in a manner that (a) uses the skill criteria and (b) feels authentic for the trainee. **Example counselor responses for each client context are provided at the end of this exercise. Trainees should attempt to improvise their own responses before reading the examples.**

BEGINNER-LEVEL CLIENT CONTEXTS FOR EXERCISE 8
Beginner Client Context 1
The client decided to engage in career counseling because they are unhappy in their current job. A few suggested career paths are sales force developer, tenure-track professor, and human resources (HR) manager.
Beginner Client Context 2
The client decided to engage in career counseling because they want to decide on a college major within the next month. Assessment results suggest career paths of interest may be a chef, a photographer, or a creative writer.
Beginner Client Context 3
The client decided to engage in career counseling because they are interviewing with three potential employers and are undecided as to which organization may be the best fit for them. The assessment results suggest career paths of interest might include a freelance writer, a freelance photographer, or a personal trainer.
Beginner Client Context 4
The client decided to pursue career counseling because they are not happy in their current major, and they would like to explore other potential majors. A few potential career paths that capitalize on their interests may include journalism, interior design, advertising, marketing, architecture, and web development.
Beginner Client Context 5
The client decided to pursue career counseling because they were recently laid off at work. The client is now considering a career transition. Careers that align for this client might include lawyer, sales manager, and lobbyist.

 Assess and adjust the difficulty before moving to the next difficulty level (see Step 3 in the exercise instructions).

INTERMEDIATE-LEVEL CLIENT CONTEXTS FOR EXERCISE 8
Intermediate Client Context 1
The client decided to pursue career counseling because they are graduating from high school in a few months and would like to consider a range of career options. According to their career assessment results, some career paths of potential interest include photographer, web designer, economist, and researcher.
Intermediate Client Context 2
The client decided to pursue career counseling because they want to engage in greater self-awareness and pursue a career path that aligns with their values. Assessment results suggest that a few relevant career paths might include graphic designer, game designer, and event manager.
Intermediate Client Context 3
The client decided to pursue career counseling because they feel unchallenged in their current work environment and would like to consider alternative career paths. Some related careers include computer programmer, quality assurance and compliance officer, editor, and data analyst.
Intermediate Client Context 4
The client decided to pursue career counseling because they are feeling pressure from their parents to pursue a degree in medicine, but they are failing their pre-med courses. A few related careers include sales manager, lawyer, architectural manager, or judge.
Intermediate Client Context 5
The client decided to pursue career counseling because their current job feels stagnant, and they would like to consider alternative career paths. A few proposed career paths are air traffic controller, professor, computer scientist, and police officer.

🛈 **Assess and adjust the difficulty before moving to the next difficulty level (see Step 3 in the exercise instructions).**

ADVANCED-LEVEL CLIENT CONTEXTS FOR EXERCISE 8
Advanced Client Context 1
The client decided to engage in career counseling because they are unhappy in their current major, media and journalism. Results from a skills assessment suggest that one potential career path as a journalist.
Advanced Client Context 2
The client decided to engage in career counseling because they are graduating soon and are wondering what questions they should ask at job interviews to assess fit between their skill set and the company's needs. Some related careers include human resources manager, consultant, and market researcher.
Advanced Client Context 3
The client decided to engage in career counseling because they are pursuing a master's degree in clinical mental health counseling but are unsure what career path they would like to pursue with this degree. The assessment results suggest the client may be interested in pursuing a career as a clinical mental health counselor or human rights lawyer.
Advanced Client Context 4
The client decided to engage in career counseling because the client is feeling pressured to pursue a degree in law from their parents but does not believe they are competent to pursue this path and feel generally worn down and tired. A few careers that may be of interest include writer, public speaker, or editor.
Advanced Client Context 5
The client decided to pursue career counseling because they are trying to decide between two college majors: statistics and psychology. Results from a skills assessment suggest they may excel in programming, but the client has explicitly stated that they do not want to follow their parents' career path, which, ironically, is computer programming.

 Assess and adjust the difficulty here (see Step 3 in the exercise instructions). If appropriate, follow the instructions to make the exercise even more challenging (see Appendix A).

Example Counselor Responses: Exploring Underlying Themes in Assessments

Remember: Trainees should attempt to improvise their own responses before reading the examples. **Do not read the following responses verbatim unless you are having trouble coming up with your own!**

EXAMPLE RESPONSES TO BEGINNER-LEVEL CLIENT CONTEXTS FOR EXERCISE 8

Example Response to Beginner Client Context 1

Your assessment report suggested a range of career paths that may be of interest to you, including sales force developer, tenure-track professor, and HR manager. On the surface, these specific career paths may—or may not!—interest you. So let's take a moment to dig a little deeper and explore themes that might connect the career paths together. (Criterion 1) One thing that strikes me as I look at these jobs is that they all seem to involve opportunities for advancement. (Criterion 2) I wonder if career advancement might be an important career feature for you? (Criterion 3)

Example Response to Beginner Client Context 2

The results of your career assessment suggest you may be interested in careers as a chef, photographer, or creative writer, but these are just a few of many career paths that might interest you. (Criterion 1) In considering interest areas that might connect these careers together, I sense these careers may represent underlying interests in self-expression and creativity. (Criterion 2) I wonder if exploring careers that foster and support creativity would be important to you? (Criterion 3)

Example Response to Beginner Client Context 3

Interestingly, your assessment results seem to highlight a range of potential careers of interest, many of which are in the freelance area. Let's spend a moment exploring options that may be a good fit for you. (Criterion 1) Given that freelance positions were ranked highly in your assessment results, I wonder if this might highlight a potential interest of yours in flexible careers that allow for work–life balance. (Criterion 2) And because you want to enter your upcoming interviews with intentionality, I wonder if asking prospective employers about their company culture, what a typical day looks like on the job, and their policies on remote or hybrid working could be useful? (Criterion 3)

Example Response to Beginner Client Context 4

Let's turn our attention to your assessment results for a moment. I'd love to chat with you about what the results suggest. Keep in mind that while the specific majors may (or may not) interest you, there may be an underlying theme that does. We'll explore that together. (Criterion 1) One thing that struck me as I read your interest in areas like journalism, interior design, and architecture is that all these majors often require an imaginative, creative, and open mind. (Criterion 2) I wonder if creativity is an important value of yours. Do you, or have you, engaged in any creative hobbies? If so, what was that like for you? (Criterion 3)

Example Response to Beginner Client Context 5

Let's chat a bit about options for career transitions. It should be noted that the assessment report provides some suggestions related to careers that may be of interest to you but only represent a few of many careers that could be a good fit. Some careers include lawyer, sales manager, and lobbyist. (Criterion 1) I wonder if a few themes that may connect careers in law, sales, and lobbying could be that they all require assertiveness and energy? (Criterion 2) How much do you enjoy working in settings that capitalize on utilizing your energy and assertiveness? (Criterion 3)

Exploring Underlying Themes in Assessments

EXAMPLE RESPONSES TO INTERMEDIATE-LEVEL CLIENT CONTEXTS FOR EXERCISE 8

Example Response to Intermediate Client Context 1

Let's spend the next few minutes delving into your career assessment results! The results suggested a number of career paths that may be of interest to you, like photographer, web designer, economist, or researcher, but some of those specific jobs may—or may not—really appeal to you. (Criterion 1) What I'd like for us to do next is spend some time looking at the thread that ties those jobs together. One of the things that stood out to me when I thought about these jobs is that they seem to involve working independently. (Criterion 2) I wonder if that fits for you: How much do you see yourself enjoying, or not enjoying, working independently? (Criterion 3)

Example Response to Intermediate Client Context 2

I'm excited to talk with you about your career assessment results; we have a lot to discuss! While the report suggests some potential career paths, like graphic designer, game designer, and event manager, what I'd really like to focus on with you is the theme that underlies them, because that may also suggest other careers that could be a good fit for you. (Criterion 1) I wonder if the career assessment is picking up on your value of creativity? (Criterion 2) To what degree do you hope your career will foster and support your creativity? (Criterion 3)

Example Response to Intermediate Client Context 3

Let's delve into your assessment results! You might notice that the assessment report suggests you may be particularly drawn to certain careers like computer programmer, quality assurance and compliance officer, editor, and data analyst, but instead of specific job titles, let's start by uncovering the underlying theme that ties these jobs together. (Criterion 1) As I was reviewing your report, one potential theme I noticed was that each of these careers requires a high level of attention to detail. (Criterion 2) When you think about your ideal career, do you like focusing on the bigger picture or enjoy exploring details and specifics? (Criterion 3)

Example Response to Intermediate Client Context 4

Your assessment results suggest you might be interested in a range of careers, including sales manager, lawyer, architectural manager, or judge, but what I'd like for us to start with is uncovering the theme that might encompass this range of careers. From there, we can narrow down some careers that might be best suited to you. (Criterion 1) As we start, I wonder if the report might be picking up on your skills of influencing others, or maybe an interest in critical decision making. (Criterion 2) To what degree do you enjoy either leading others or being a decision maker in the work that you do? (Criterion 3)

Example Response to Intermediate Client Context 5

I know your current job has been feeling quite stale, so let's spend some time looking at other potential careers that could be a good fit. Your assessment report suggests some specific careers, but keep in mind that those careers represent only a few of many career paths that could potentially be a good fit for you. (Criterion 1) Let's take a moment to look at what themes might be under the surface of these career paths. When I look at the range of career paths listed in your report, what strikes me is that each of these careers seems to involve critical thinking and addressing challenges. (Criterion 2) I wonder if a career that involves significant critical thinking might be particularly rewarding for you? (Criterion 3)

EXAMPLE RESPONSES TO ADVANCED-LEVEL CLIENT CONTEXTS FOR EXERCISE 8
Example Response to Advanced Client Context 1
I know one of the reasons why you took this career assessment was to explore careers outside of your current major in media and journalism, so you may be surprised to see that the report suggests that journalism may be an area of interest for you. Let's dig a bit deeper because I wonder if the report is really picking up on some underlying interests for you. (Criterion 1) Could this report be picking up on your skills in writing and creative endeavors? (Criterion 2) What are your thoughts about exploring other majors and careers that involve creativity and self-expression? (Criterion 3)
Example Response to Advanced Client Context 2
Let's focus on your career assessment results! Keep in mind that these careers represent only a few of many that may interest you. For that reason, we'll start by looking at the theme that connects each of these careers together. (Criterion 1) I wonder if a theme connecting HR manager, consultant, and market researcher, for example, might relate to your interest in collaboration and working in teams. (Criterion 2) To what degree would you find teamwork important in your new career? I wonder if it could be helpful to ask each of your prospective employers about the degree and types of collaboration involved in each job? (Criterion 3)
Example Response to Advanced Client Context 3
Perhaps unsurprisingly, the results suggested you may be interested in a career as a clinical mental health counselor, but keep in mind that's only one potential career that may be of interest to you. (Criterion 1) While a profession as a counselor is rather broad, what I found interesting is that it also suggested an interest in human rights and perhaps a value of social justice. (Criterion 2) To what degree would you find incorporating social justice in your daily work important? (Criterion 3)
Example Response to Advanced Client Context 4
The results of your assessment suggest you may be interested in career paths including writing, public speaking, or editing. However, it's important to keep in mind that these career paths are just a few of many that could be a fit for you. (Criterion 1) Although those very specific career paths may not be of interest to you, they may represent an underlying career theme that could itself be a good fit. So let's pause for a moment and reflect on the underlying theme or themes these careers may represent: One thing that struck me as I saw those three careers in your report was that they all tend to involve skills in self-expression, creativity, and/or organization. (Criterion 2) I wonder if any of those attributes are areas you feel you have strengths or an interest in? (Criterion 3)
Example Response to Advanced Client Context 5
You might be surprised to hear that your assessment results suggested an interest in computer programming. However, this is only one of many career paths that the assessment report suggests for you, and rather than focusing on the assessment as a prescription for careers you should pursue, what I'd like to do is start by exploring a theme that underlies different careers conveyed in the report to help you find a good career fit. (Criterion 1) I wonder if the report is picking up on an interest in problem solving, analytical skills, and detail orientation? (Criterion 2) To what degree are those skill sets important to you in a future career? (Criterion 3)

Addressing Client Ambivalence and Skepticism

Preparations for Exercise 9

1. Read the instructions in Chapter 2.
2. Download the Deliberate Practice Reaction Form and the Deliberate Practice Diary Form at https://www.apa.org/pubs/books/deliberate-practice-career-counseling (see the "Resources" tab; also available in Appendixes A and B, respectively).

Skill Description

Skill Difficulty Level: Advanced

Clients engage in career counseling sessions for a variety of reasons. Some clients pursue career counseling because they want to explore options for college majors or careers after completing their degrees; some enter career counseling because they want to pursue a new career path; some engage in career counseling because they are tired, worn down, unsatisfied, or unfulfilled with their current path; some seek out career counseling with hopes for support in the midst of difficult, even discriminatory, work situations.

Some enter career counseling through their own volition, but others enter because they have been encouraged to do so by others. Some approach career counseling sessions optimistic about the potential benefits of the process, and some enter with significant reluctance or because someone else (e.g., a parent, significant other, colleague, friend) encouraged them to try it out.

Clients who enter career counseling excited and hopeful about the process are often engaged in the career counseling sessions, homework, and self-reflection. But what about clients who enter begrudgingly, guardedly, or hesitantly? These clients can make even seasoned career counselors anxious. In a sense, it may feel counterintuitive for career

---

https://doi.org/10.1037/0000442-011

Deliberate Practice in Career Counseling, by J. M. Taylor, A. Vaz, and T. Rousmaniere

Copyright © 2025 by the American Psychological Association. All rights reserved.

counselors to engage in career counseling with a client who does not necessarily want to be there. Because of this, we have dedicated Exercise 9 to working with clients who may be your most challenging: the ambivalent or skeptical career counseling clients.

As you think about ambivalent clients, it may be useful to consider them through the same stage of change lens (Prochaska & DiClemente, 1983) used to view clients engaged in motivational interviewing or personal counseling. Understanding your client's current stage of change can give you a window into their motivations for engaging in career counseling and their commitment to the process. Using this model, this exercise focuses on the precontemplation stage (e.g., the stage in which clients have not yet acknowledged there is an issue that needs to be addressed) and the contemplation stage (e.g., the stage in which clients acknowledge there is an issue but are not yet ready or sure that they can or want to make a change).

When experiencing ambivalent or skeptical clients, career counselors are encouraged to "roll with resistance" (Manuel et al., 2022; Schumacher & Madson, 2014). To do so, first, validate the client's concerns or perspective on the issue that brought them to career counseling. This requires listening closely to their experiences, their body language, and the intonation of their voice, empathizing with their emotions and experiences and helping them feel seen and heard.

It is important to acknowledge that change (e.g., changing majors, changing careers, losing a job, trying something new) might evoke feelings of unease in certain clients. This exercise encourages clients to explore how a change that initially seems intimidating could potentially lead to positive outcomes. The apprehension of embracing change or venturing into new territories can sometimes halt clients' progress, giving rise to mixed feelings or a guarded stance that may resemble skepticism. This exercise, from our perspective, serves as an opportunity for clients to embrace the concept of uncertainty, welcome optimism, and contemplate new beginnings and alternative viewpoints.

The second step involves inviting your client to self-reflect by asking them an open-ended question that encourages them to explore their "why" for career counseling. You might ask your client what the drawbacks could be of them not exploring their issues in career counseling. You could invite the client to imagine their goals for the future and what, in particular, might differ in their imagined future life from their current life experiences. You could also encourage the client to consider their reasons for wanting a particular change in their current career path.

Note that when using this skill set, the goal is not to convince the client why they should engage in career counseling or pursue a certain path. Rather, the goal in this exercise is to invite your client to explore both sides of their motivation and to consider the implications of specific actions or inactions.

To summarize, using this skill set, the counselor should improvise a response to each client statement following these skill criteria:

1. **Validate the client's concern or perspective on the presenting topic.** Validating your client's concerns or perspectives is a critical first step in building rapport and trust with your client and will help your client feel heard and understood. This can be a particularly helpful technique to employ before inviting your client to explore their issue from a different angle, as evidenced in step 2:

2. **Ask an open-ended question about the following:**
   - **Option A:** The downsides to not working on their presenting issue.
   - **Option B:** How the client would like things to be different.
   - **Option C:** Why the client might want to change.

Addressing Client Ambivalence and Skepticism

This second step involves inviting your client to explore their concerns through a different lens. If your client is ambivalent or concerned about working on a presenting issue, instead of trying to "convince" them why they should work on the issue, gently invite them to explore the implications, if any, of not working on the issue. If their skepticism relates to pursuing something different in relation to their career, this step involves asking them to imagine what life would look like if they did not change directions or their current course, how they might like things to look different, or what motivations or interests they have related to pursuing a different path. (For more skill-building exercises related to this topic, see Manuel et al., 2022.)

Note. Feel free to choose any option to fulfill Criterion 2, but we encourage you to alternate your response options so that you do not over rely on one technique to the detriment of the others.

SKILL CRITERIA FOR EXERCISE 9

1. Validate the client's concern or perspective on the presenting topic.
2. Ask an open-ended question about the following:
   - Option A: The downsides to not working on their presenting issue.
   - Option B: How the client would like things to be different.
   - Option C: Why the client might want to change.

Examples of Counselors Addressing Client Ambivalence and Skepticism

Example 1

CLIENT: [*frustrated*] What's the point of even talking with you about changing my job? I think this may be a waste of time. Sure, I hate my job, but I just don't see what I can do about it. I've put up with this job for 15 years now—I guess I can put up with it longer.

COUNSELOR: It makes a lot of sense that you feel defeated after being stuck in a job you don't like for so long. (Criterion 1) From your perspective, would there be any downsides to not discussing a potential job change? (Criterion 2, Option A)

or

And yet, it sounds like you're pretty frustrated with where you're at. How would you like things to be different career-wise? (Criterion 2, Option B)

or

Just so I get a clearer picture, from your perspective, why would you want to change your current job situation? (Criterion 2, Option C)

Example 2

CLIENT: [*perturbed*] My partner wanted me to come to career counseling because he said the stress I bring home from work is impacting our relationship. But I don't know—I don't think it's a really big deal.

COUNSELOR: I hear in your voice that it's been frustrating to hear your partner tie your professional life, the stressors at work, to your personal life, your relationship with your partner. From your perspective, the issues don't really seem like a big deal. (Criterion 1) Would there be any potential repercussions or consequences to not exploring your stress with your job in here? (Criterion 2, Option A)

or

What things, big or small—anything or nothing—would you like to change with your current job? (Criterion 2, Option B)

or

What reasons, if any, would you have for wanting to make a change with your current job situation? (Criterion 2, Option C)

Example 3

CLIENT: [*despondent*] I'm not even quite sure why I'm here. I don't really think I have much to offer a job—my skills are really limited. I sent off 15 job applications last week, and I've gotten 15 rejections.

COUNSELOR: I understand. Rejections are never easy, especially when we're working hard to make a change. It can make anyone feel like giving up, just so we don't have to risk rejection again. (Criterion 1) If we didn't explore your career options and professional skills in here, what might happen? What, if any, downsides could there be to not exploring your career in here? (Criterion 2, Option A)

or

If the job hunt looked different for you, how would it ideally differ from what you're experiencing right now? (Criterion 2, Option B)

or

Given that the process has been so discouraging, what are some reasons why you might want to be here in career counseling? (Criterion 2, Option C)

INSTRUCTIONS FOR EXERCISE 9

Step 1: Role-Play and Feedback

- The client says the first beginner client statement. The counselor **improvises** a response based on the skill criteria.
- The trainer (or, if not available, the client) provides **brief** feedback based on the skill criteria.
- The client then repeats the same statement, and the counselor again improvises a response. The trainer (or client) again provides brief feedback.

Step 2: Repeat

- Repeat Step 1 for all the statements **in the current difficulty level** (beginner, intermediate, or advanced).

Step 3: Assess and Adjust Difficulty

- The counselor completes the Deliberate Practice Reaction Form (see Appendix A) and decides whether to make the exercise easier or harder or to repeat the same difficulty level.

Step 4: Repeat for Approximately 15 Minutes

- Repeat Steps 1 to 3 for at least 15 minutes.
- The trainees then switch counselor and client roles and start over.

> **Now it's your turn! Follow Steps 1 and 2 from the instructions.**

Remember: The goal of the role-play is for trainees to practice improvising responses to the client statements in a manner that (a) uses the skill criteria and (b) feels authentic for the trainee. **Example counselor responses for each client statement are provided at the end of this exercise. Trainees should attempt to improvise their own responses before reading the examples.**

BEGINNER-LEVEL CLIENT STATEMENTS FOR EXERCISE 9
Beginner Client Statement 1
[Worried] I'm failing my classes. I know this major isn't really a good fit for me, but I'm really scared to try something different.
Beginner Client Statement 2
[Irked] So I'll be taking career assessments? I've already tried a lot of things in here, and I don't see how a test would be all that useful.
Beginner Client Statement 3
[Insecure] I want to open up to you in our sessions and share, but I'm afraid you might judge me.
Beginner Client Statement 4
[Defeated] Maybe I'm never going to advance at work. I don't know what the point of even trying is anymore.
Beginner Client Statement 5
[Discouraged] I always come to work early and leave late. I'm so tired at the end of each day, but I don't really think I can talk to my supervisor about it. What if they just think I'm complaining?

> **Assess and adjust the difficulty before moving to the next difficulty level (see Step 3 in the exercise instructions).**

INTERMEDIATE-LEVEL CLIENT STATEMENTS FOR EXERCISE 9

Intermediate Client Statement 1

[Disheartened] I've thought about applying for a new job, but . . . I don't know. It seems really daunting.

Intermediate Client Statement 2

[Discouraged] I hate my job. It doesn't feel meaningful—I'm just working for my paycheck. But, I guess, is there meaning in any job, really?

Intermediate Client Statement 3

[Defeated] I failed my chemistry exam. Maybe I'm just not cut out for college.

Intermediate Client Statement 4

[Embarrassed] I've gotten rejected from every job interview I've had so far. I don't even know what the point is of trying anymore.

Intermediate Client Statement 5

[Disengaged] I've thought about changing my major, but I don't even know what else I'd do if I wasn't in political science. Both of my parents are in poli-sci.

 Assess and adjust the difficulty before moving to the next difficulty level (see Step 3 in the exercise instructions).

ADVANCED-LEVEL CLIENT STATEMENTS FOR EXERCISE 9

Advanced Client Statement 1

[**Discouraged**] My boss makes sexist comments about me nearly every day. It's so messed up. And yet, the entire team hears her, and she's had zero repercussions for it. I would say something, but I'm afraid of retaliation. I don't think things will ever change, so why even talk about it here?

Advanced Client Statement 2

[**Checked out**] I don't know what I'm even doing here. I don't think anything will really help me.

Advanced Client Statement 3

[**Confused**] I feel stuck in a dead-end career. Sure, it puts food on the table, but maybe I could provide for my family better if I explored other career options. But then again, if I did, it feels like such a risk. I don't really know what to do.

Advanced Client Statement 4

[**Hurt**] I'm not really sure if I want to talk about how the messages from my family have influenced my career decision making. My experiences with them growing up were pretty painful, and my dad left us when I was 4 years old.

Advanced Client Statement 5

[**Downtrodden**] I've always wanted to go to college, but my husband told me he'd rather I stay at home and take care of our children. He thinks me going to college would distract me from being a good mother.

✋ **Assess and adjust the difficulty here (see Step 3 in the exercise instructions). If appropriate, follow the instructions to make the exercise even more challenging (see Appendix A).**

Example Counselor Responses: Addressing Client Ambivalence and Skepticism

Remember: Trainees should attempt to improvise their own responses before reading the examples. **Do not read the following responses verbatim unless you are having trouble coming up with your own!**

EXAMPLE RESPONSES TO BEGINNER-LEVEL CLIENT STATEMENTS FOR EXERCISE 9
Example Response to Beginner Client Statement 1
Change can feel so scary! (Criterion 1) What would be the downsides, if any, to not trying something different? (Criterion 2, Option A)
Example Response to Beginner Client Statement 2
I get it. Your time is valuable, and you don't want to waste it with something that may not pay off. (Criterion 1) If we did things differently here in career counseling, how would you want to spend our time in here? (Criterion 2, Option B)
Example Response to Beginner Client Statement 3
I understand. It's difficult to open up to others, especially if there's a concern the other person might judge us. (Criterion 1) If you were to speak from the part of you that wants to open up and share, what would that side say? What, if any, benefits would there be to opening up in here? (Criterion 2, Option C)
Example Response to Beginner Client Statement 4
I hear how discouraging this has been. It sounds like you've been trying to advance at work, but you're not seeing the rewards from it. (Criterion 1) What might some of the downsides be if we didn't explore your feeling of "stuckness" at work in here? (Criterion 2, Option A)
Example Response to Beginner Client Statement 5
I can understand how burned out you might feel! Part of you wants to find a better balance, but part of you sounds scared that you may be misperceived at work if you do. (Criterion 1) If you were able to talk with your supervisor and found a better work–life balance, what might life look like for you? How would you feel? What would life after work look like? (Criterion 2, Option B)

EXAMPLE RESPONSES TO INTERMEDIATE-LEVEL CLIENT STATEMENTS FOR EXERCISE 9
Example Response to Intermediate Client Statement 1
It can feel really overwhelming to apply for new jobs. (Criterion 1) If you didn't apply for a new job, what, if anything, would you potentially lose? What would be the downsides of not applying for a new job? (Criterion 2, Option A)
Example Response to Intermediate Client Statement 2
I hear you. You want to feel like you're making an impact in your job, and your current job isn't providing that to you. It sounds like you're also wondering if there really is meaning in work. (Criterion 1) If you could invite yourself to imagine, what would a meaningful job look like to you? How would it look different from what you currently do? (Criterion 2, Option B)
Example Response to Intermediate Client Statement 3
I imagine that felt so disappointing, and disappointments can certainly make anyone feel like giving up. (Criterion 1) What reasons, if any, might there be for you not giving up? Why might you want to stay in school? (Criterion 2, Option C)
Example Response to Intermediate Client Statement 4
Rejection can definitely make anyone feel like no longer trying. (Criterion 1) Let's unpack that a bit more: What would be the downsides of not trying some new approaches to the job interview process that we could otherwise explore in our career counseling sessions? (Criterion 2, Option A)
Example Response to Intermediate Client Statement 5
It's difficult to even consider changing a major when it's what we've known for so much of our lives and when it's what we've been exposed to so much. (Criterion 1) If you were to contrast political science with other majors, what do you like least about political science or most about other majors you're considering? (Criterion 2, Option B)

EXAMPLE RESPONSES TO ADVANCED-LEVEL CLIENT STATEMENTS FOR EXERCISE 9

Example Response to Advanced Client Statement 1

That is so messed up! It must have felt very discouraging and disempowering. (Criterion 1) If nothing changes, what might the next 5 years in your job look like? (Criterion 2, Option A)

Example Response to Advanced Client Statement 2

I imagine it's felt really discouraging to come into these sessions and not feel like they are helping. (Criterion 1) If you were to stay in career counseling, what would you hope it would look like? (Criterion 2, Option B)

Example Response to Advanced Client Statement 3

I hear the tension you're feeling between staying in your current job that provides the basic needs for your family or taking a risk with a different career path that might provide better for them in the future. (Criterion 1) You mentioned that a new career path could help you provide better for your family in the future. What are some other reasons, if any, for considering pursuing a different career path? (Criterion 2, Option C)

Example Response to Advanced Client Statement 4

I get it and am grateful that you let me know this. Families can be so complicated, and memories can be painful. (Criterion 1) From your perspective, what, if any, potential downsides would there be to not talking about your family's influence on your career decision making and values? (Criterion 2, Option A)

Example Response to Advanced Client Statement 5

It can feel so paralyzing to try to make a decision when our wants differ from what others want from us, especially when those people are so significant in our lives. (Criterion 1) Let's focus first on your interest in going to college: What are some reasons why you'd like to go to college? (Criterion 2, Option C)

Assigning Homework in Career Counseling

EXERCISE 10

Preparations for Exercise 10

1. Read the instructions in Chapter 2.
2. Download the Deliberate Practice Reaction Form and the Deliberate Practice Diary Form at https://www.apa.org/pubs/books/deliberate-practice-career-counseling (see the "Resources" tab; also available in Appendixes A and B, respectively).

Skill Description

Skill Difficulty Level: Advanced

Providing clients with homework activities encourages them to continue engaging in career counseling in between sessions, fosters career counseling progress, provides additional opportunities to process insights at later career counseling sessions, and encourages clients to be actively involved in their career counseling experience. You will find that some clients are drawn to homework and feel more invested in career counseling when they engage in work in between sessions, while others may find the idea of "homework" burdensome or boring.

Perhaps the single most important part of inviting clients to engage in homework involves actively listening to them and tailoring the homework activities, and the time involved in the homework itself, based on the client's needs, the topics you are covering in the session, and the client's goals. If a client does not have much time to invest in exploring their careers outside of a session, you might suggest an activity that could be done in 15 to 20 minutes. Here are a few examples:

- Complete the O*Net Interest Profiler (https://www.mynextmove.org/explore/ip) or O*Net Work Importance Locator (https://www.onetcenter.org/WIL.html).

---

https://doi.org/10.1037/0000442-012

Deliberate Practice in Career Counseling, by J. M. Taylor, A. Vaz, and T. Rousmaniere

Copyright © 2025 by the American Psychological Association. All rights reserved.

- Gather information about specific careers of interest. A few online resources include the Occupational Outlook Handbook (https://www.bls.gov/ooh) and MyPlan (https://www.myplan.com/).
- Develop a draft resume or cover letter to review in the next career counseling session.
- Join an online professional networking group.
- Join a professional association.
- Engage in an activity that promotes work-life balance.

Alternatively, if your client is interested in delving in deeper to explore career options or has more time to do so than the previously mentioned clients, here are a few additional homework activities you might offer:

- Contact others who are successful in fields of interest and engage in informational interviews to learn more about their careers.
- Take a college, lifelong learning, or technical course to begin learning a new skill and to explore interest engagement.
- Engage in job shadowing.
- Find a mentor (e.g., join professional networks, contact professors, contact colleagues).
- Delve into an area of interest (e.g., contact a professor to inquire about any available teaching or research assistant positions).
- Attend a conference to network.
- Earn a microcertificate.
- Ask for feedback from colleagues, supervisors, mentors, and trusted loved ones about one's skills and talents.

To assign homework in a session, the counselor should improvise a response to each client statement following these skill criteria:

1. **Suggest a homework activity.** In this step, you will offer a gentle suggestion for a homework activity, as relevant to the client's overall goals and as relevant to the topic(s) you and your client are currently processing in career counseling.

2. **Invite the client to share their thoughts or reactions about your suggestion.** In this step, you will encourage your client to discuss with you their thoughts about your suggested homework. This is an especially important step because it allows you to put your finger on the pulse of your client's reactions to your suggestions, any hesitations they have about completing the homework, whether they "buy into" the importance of it, and what barriers they might face in relation to completing it.

SKILL CRITERIA FOR EXERCISE 10

1. Suggest a homework activity.
2. Invite the client to share their thoughts or reactions about your suggestion.

Examples of Counselors Using the Skill of Assigning Homework

Example 1

CLIENT: [*stressed*] My guidance counselor told me that I have to decide on a major by the end of the semester, but how am I supposed to figure that out?! I'm thinking of either medicine or law, but I don't know. . . . My aunt is a doctor, and her job sounds really interesting, but my cousin just made partner at his law firm, which sounds really cool too.

COUNSELOR: Because you know people who are both doctors and lawyers, perhaps it would be helpful to conduct a focused informational interview with each of them to learn more about a day in their life. (Criterion 1) What are your thoughts about conducting interviews with each of them? (Criterion 2)

Example 2

CLIENT: [*nervous*] I'm going on the job market soon, but it seems like you have to know the right people to get a job in my field. I don't even know where to begin!

COUNSELOR: I wonder if a professional conference might be one way to network and get to know others in your field. (Criterion 1) What are your thoughts about going to a conference? (Criterion 2)

Example 3

CLIENT: [*overwhelmed*] I'm so tired and stressed all the time. I just feel so burned out at work—I don't take any breaks and I'm often working up through 11 at night. Even so, I still can't get caught up. Do you have any ideas about how I could deal with this?

COUNSELOR: I hear your heart saying that you need rest, a lunch break, and a more reasonable hour that you can clock out of work for the evening. It sounds like you might need tighter boundaries around your work hours to help with what might otherwise turn into burnout. (Criterion 1) What would happen if you set greater boundaries around your work hours? (Criterion 2)

INSTRUCTIONS FOR EXERCISE 10
Step 1: Role-Play and Feedback
- The client says the first beginner client statement. The counselor **improvises** a response based on the skill criteria.
- The trainer (or, if not available, the client) provides **brief** feedback based on the skill criteria.
- The client then repeats the same statement, and the counselor again improvises a response. The trainer (or client) again provides brief feedback.
Step 2: Repeat
- Repeat Step 1 for all the statements **in the current difficulty level** (beginner, intermediate, or advanced).
Step 3: Assess and Adjust Difficulty
- The counselor completes the Deliberate Practice Reaction Form (see Appendix A) and decides whether to make the exercise easier or harder or to repeat the same difficulty level.
Step 4: Repeat for Approximately 15 Minutes
- Repeat Steps 1 to 3 for at least 15 minutes.
- The trainees then switch counselor and client roles and start over.

Now it's your turn! Follow Steps 1 and 2 from the instructions.

Remember: The goal of the role-play is for trainees to practice improvising responses to the client statements in a manner that (a) uses the skill criteria and (b) feels authentic for the trainee. **Example counselor responses for each client statement are provided at the end of this exercise. Trainees should attempt to improvise their own responses before reading the examples.**

BEGINNER-LEVEL CLIENT STATEMENTS FOR EXERCISE 10
Beginner Client Statement 1
[Depressed] I just don't think I'm good at much of anything. I mean, how can I decide on a career if I have no skills? What skills do I really have anyway?
Beginner Client Statement 2
[Confused] There are so many things I'm interested in! I really don't know how to narrow my career options down.
Beginner Client Statement 3
[Stressed] I'm considering a career in the field of science, but I don't know which science discipline to pursue. There are so many options, and I don't even know where to start. I'm still in my freshman year of college, but I'm hoping to declare a major soon. I'd love some suggestions for things I can do to get some greater clarity on my path.
Beginner Client Statement 4
[Curious] I've always wanted to be a physician, but I'm not sure I want to invest in that much more schooling. Plus, I have kids to feed, and I'm worried about what my student loan debt would look like coming out of 4 years of medical school plus a residency and maybe a fellowship. How could I find similar careers that don't require so much schooling?
Beginner Client Statement 5
[Inquisitive] I think I might like teaching high schoolers, but I'm not sure. I've never done it before, and I don't know if I'd be any good at it.

 Assess and adjust the difficulty before moving to the next difficulty level (see Step 3 in the exercise instructions).

INTERMEDIATE-LEVEL CLIENT STATEMENTS FOR EXERCISE 10
Intermediate Client Statement 1
[Curious] How can I find a career that aligns with my purpose and what's important to me in life?
Intermediate Client Statement 2
[Upset] My career is so stressful. I never have enough hours in the day. How can I reasonably get everything done that's required in this role?! I feel like I've been set up to fail.
Intermediate Client Statement 3
[Overwhelmed] I'd really like to go to college, but I don't think it's an option for me. It's too expensive, and I don't want to take out loans.
Intermediate Client Statement 4
[Timid] I think it would be cool to join a science lab here at the university, but I feel awkward asking someone to join their lab—the professors here are some of the best in the field.
Intermediate Client Statement 5
[Anxious] I have my first job interview in 2 weeks! I'm so nervous! How can I prepare for the interview? Tell me all your tips!

 Assess and adjust the difficulty before moving to the next difficulty level (see Step 3 in the exercise instructions).

ADVANCED-LEVEL CLIENT STATEMENTS FOR EXERCISE 10
Advanced Client Statement 1
[Frustrated] I feel like we keep going in circles here! I'm not sure career counseling is even helping me. I already know that I want to go into the health care field, but I still don't know what specific career path to pursue once I graduate from this university. I don't even know enough about all my career options to make this decision.
Advanced Client Statement 2
[Sad] I just lost my job. I don't even know where to start looking for another one. In fact, I don't even know who I am anymore, if I'm not a teacher.
Advanced Client Statement 3
[Worried] I just finished my job interview. I think it went well, but they are interviewing multiple candidates for the job. They told me over a hundred candidates applied, and they are interviewing their top 10. I just don't know how I could possibly stand out from the rest of the candidates!
Advanced Client Statement 4
[Disheartened] I've been so lonely since I retired from my job. I'm not quite sure what to do.
Advanced Client Statement 5
[Frazzled] I am so tired and stressed. I'm a single parent, trying my best to care for my four children, all while working 7 days a week between my two jobs. I don't know how much longer I can do this. I need a change. I wish I knew how to ask for a raise or more reasonable work hours.

 Assess and adjust the difficulty here (see Step 3 in the exercise instructions). If appropriate, follow the instructions to make the exercise even more challenging (see Appendix A).

Example Counselor Responses: Assigning Homework in Career Counseling

Remember: Trainees should attempt to improvise their own responses before reading the examples. **Do not read the following responses verbatim unless you are having trouble coming up with your own!**

EXAMPLE RESPONSES TO BEGINNER-LEVEL CLIENT STATEMENTS FOR EXERCISE 10
Example Response to Beginner Client Statement 1
Sometimes it's hard for us to see or acknowledge our strengths, and sometimes it can be useful to hear perspectives from others outside of ourselves—those who can see us from a different lens. I wonder what three people you trust would say about the strengths and qualities they admire most in you. If you asked three people this weekend what they believe your top strengths are, I'd be curious to see what themes you might notice as a result and how that might relate to different career options you're considering. (Criterion 1) What are your thoughts about trying that out this weekend? (Criterion 2)
Example Response to Beginner Client Statement 2
Perhaps we can start to clear the fog you feel you're in by identifying your top interest areas. Before the next session, I'd love for you to take the Strong Interest Inventory, and then when you come to our next session, we can discuss the results. (Criterion 1) What are your thoughts about us starting there? (Criterion 2)
Example Response to Beginner Client Statement 3
I wonder if it would be helpful to approach this semester through the lens of curiosity and open-mindedness. Given that you're still in your freshman year and have some room to explore your interests before having to declare a major, perhaps it could be useful to take a course in chemistry, another in physics, and another in biology, in the spring to compare and contrast these interest areas further. (Criterion 1) How does that sound? (Criterion 2)
Example Response to Beginner Client Statement 4
One idea could be to check out the Occupational Outlook Handbook online this weekend. You can type in a keyword, like "physician," and pull up their webpage on physicians. In one of the tabs, there's an option for "Similar Occupations," and you could start exploring some similar careers from there. (Criterion 1) What are your thoughts about starting there to widen your career considerations outside of a career as a physician? (Criterion 2)
Example Response to Beginner Client Statement 5
Yes, it's hard to know what we're drawn to until sometimes we try things out. I wonder if trying out substitute teaching on an occasional basis or volunteering with a school might give you a better sense of your interest in this area. (Criterion 1) Would that be something of interest to you? (Criterion 2)

EXAMPLE RESPONSES TO INTERMEDIATE-LEVEL CLIENT STATEMENTS FOR EXERCISE 10

Example Response to Intermediate Client Statement 1

That's a great question. There are a lot of things we can do together in here to explore that further. One thing you could do in between our sessions involves completing an online values card sort. This will help you prioritize the values that are most important to you, so we can be thoughtful about exploring careers that align with your most salient values. These assessments usually take about 20 to 30 minutes to complete. (Criterion 1) Would that be something you'd be interested in trying out before we meet again? (Criterion 2)

Example Response to Intermediate Client Statement 2

It sounds very overwhelming. If you were to audit your weekly tasks this week, create small goals, and organize them by priority level (from most critical or urgent to least), I wonder if that might help your week feel more manageable. (Criterion 1) Would that be something you'd be willing to try out? We could check in on how it felt to try this when we meet again next week. (Criterion 2)

Example Response to Intermediate Client Statement 3

I hear you. It sounds like you'd like to go to college, but it feels unattainable and cost prohibitive. Have you explored any potential scholarships? There are several free scholarship search websites, for example, that you could explore this weekend from places like Fastweb (https://www.fastweb.com), just to see what scholarships are available. (Criterion 1) What are your thoughts about looking at scholarship options? (Criterion 2)

Example Response to Intermediate Client Statement 4

It can feel a bit intimidating to talk to others, especially if we're trying to impress them. What if you started by drafting your CV this week? When you come to our next session, we can look at your CV together and practice how you might approach a professor to ask about research opportunities. (Criterion 1) How would it feel for you if we started there? (Criterion 2)

Example Response to Intermediate Client Statement 5

Your first interview—how exciting! Let's help you get off on the right foot. Perhaps this weekend you can do two things: First, do a little research on the company you're interviewing with and jot down a few questions you have that show your interest in the work they are doing. Second, practice your responses to some of the most frequently asked interview questions, such as, "Why do you want to work with us?" and "What are your greatest strengths and greatest growth areas?" When you come to our session next week, we can do a practice run for your interviews, and I will give you feedback. (Criterion 1) How does that sound? (Criterion 2)

EXAMPLE RESPONSES TO ADVANCED-LEVEL CLIENT STATEMENTS FOR EXERCISE 10

Example Response to Advanced Client Statement 1

I get that you're feeling frustrated, and I know you're anxious to decide on a career path. Because you're not sure what career options are available in health care, maybe a reasonable starting point would be to do a little research on some of the careers in the health care field. Depending on how much time you have, you could ask informational interview questions at the next career fair at the university, targeting health care–related recruiters or you could join one of the School of Medicine's student interest groups to learn more about some of the career options in medicine. Then we could meet to discuss your thoughts and reactions to trying one of those strategies out and could consider a range of specific career options in light of your interests, skills, values, and cultural identities. (Criterion 1) Would that feel like a useful next step? (Criterion 2)

Example Response to Advanced Client Statement 2

It sounds like some identity work might be helpful. Maybe at some point between this session and our next one, you could try out this free-writing exercise: Outside of the career title, write down why you found being a teacher meaningful. Why was it important to you? Then, in our next session, we can explore ways to honor your values and purpose in this next chapter. (Criterion 1) What do you think about trying that out? (Criterion 2)

(Here is a bonus exercise you could propose.)

Maybe at some point between this session and our next one, you could try out this free-writing exercise: Start with the prompt: "I am . . ." and see what follows, allowing yourself to complete at least 15 prompts—let go of any job titles and focus on who you are as a person. Notice any themes that arise, jot down how you feel as you complete the prompts, and we can discuss it together in the next session. (Criterion 1) What do you think about trying that out? (Criterion 2)

Example Response to Advanced Client Statement 3

Perhaps it would be useful to write a short thank-you note to the interviewer. This could reiterate your interest in the position, remind them of you as a candidate and what you would bring to the position, and invite them to reach out should they have any additional questions. (Criterion 1) What are your thoughts about writing them a short note of gratitude? (Criterion 2)

Example Response to Advanced Client Statement 4

It sounds like the transition to retirement has been really challenging, and you're missing feeling connected with others. What are your thoughts about looking into volunteering opportunities? We could chat about what you've found when we meet again next time, and we could also brainstorm additional ways to help you connect with others around you. (Criterion 1) Would that be something you'd be open to trying? (Criterion 2)

Example Response to Advanced Client Statement 5

I hear how overwhelming this has been. I have an idea: between this session and our next one, I'd like for you to do some research on salary data related to your current position—that will give us ideas regarding a reasonable raise to request. Then, write down at least three accomplishments or specific actions of yours that have supported the growth of the company. When we meet together next time, we can discuss how the homework went and help you prepare to negotiate with a practice run of the negotiation process. (Criterion 1) What are your thoughts about trying this? (Criterion 2)

Annotated Career Counseling Practice Session Transcript

EXERCISE 11

It is now time to put all the skills you have learned together! This transcript is a hypothetical example of what a typical career counseling session might look like, using the skills discussed across this book. Each career counselor statement is annotated to indicate which career counseling skill from Exercises 1 through 10 is used. This transcript provides an example of how career counselors can interweave many career counseling skills in a single career counseling session.

Instructions

One trainee can play the career counselor while the other plays the client, displaying a tone and affect congruent with the material. Both participants can read line-by-line from the transcript. As with all deliberate practice, try it again! The purpose of this transcript is to provide you with an opportunity to experience how it feels to offer all the career counseling skills in the context of a session, albeit condensed, that mimics live career counseling.

> **Note to Counselors**
>
> Remember to be aware of your vocal quality. Match your tone to the client's presentation. Thus, if the client presents vulnerable, soft emotions behind their words, soften your tone to be soothing and calm. If, on the other hand, the client is aggressive and angry, match your tone to be firm and solid.

https://doi.org/10.1037/0000442-013
Deliberate Practice in Career Counseling, by J. M. Taylor, A. Vaz, and T. Rousmaniere
Copyright © 2025 by the American Psychological Association. All rights reserved.

Annotated Career Counseling Transcript

CAREER COUNSELOR 1: Hello, I'm looking forward to getting to know you! As we're starting our first session, I'd love to hear more about what brought you in for career counseling and what you hope to get out of this experience. Can we start there? (Skill 6: Setting Session Goals)

CLIENT 1: Yeah, sure. I'm finishing my first year of my pre-med major, and I'm failing all my courses. I've always wanted to be a pediatrician, but . . . I don't think it's even an option anymore. I don't even know what else I would do if I wasn't a doctor.

CAREER COUNSELOR 2: [soft, empathic tone] I imagine deciding on your major and career path has felt really stressful this semester, and maybe there's even a tinge of grief mixed in there too. I wonder if it would be helpful for us to start by exploring what drew you to medicine in the first place. Perhaps from there, we can explore your interests, skills, and values and then career paths that align for you. How would you feel about us starting there? (Skill 6: Setting Session Goals)

CLIENT 2: I guess that sounds good. [sigh] I just feel really overwhelmed. My academic advisor told me I need to decide on my major soon, so I've got to figure this out right away. To be honest, I don't even want to be here. I'm only here because my academic advisor told me it might help.

CAREER COUNSELOR 3: I get that. It sounds like you're wondering if career counseling will really be helpful. If it was helpful, what would it look like? What would you hope to get out of the process? (Skill 9: Addressing Client Ambivalence and Skepticism)

CLIENT 3: I guess I'd want to decide on my major. And maybe figure out my career path. My parents always wanted me to be a doctor. I'm worried I'll disappoint them when they find out I'm failing.

CAREER COUNSELOR 4: I hear that pressure you are feeling. You want to choose a career that will make your parents proud, and you're worried you've let them down. When you think about careers that they would be proud of, what comes to mind? (Skill 4: Exploring Your Client's Cultural and Familial Influences)

CLIENT 4: Well, we struggled a lot growing up. My parents always lived paycheck to paycheck. They don't want me to struggle like they did. And doctors—they are given so much respect for the lives they save!

CAREER COUNSELOR 5: It sounds like your parents hope for financial stability for you and a career that makes a difference on a social and individual level. How have those messages shaped the careers you've considered? (Skill 4: Exploring Your Client's Cultural and Familial Influences)

CLIENT 5: Well, I've only looked at jobs that I thought would be in demand. I don't want to struggle like they did. But I don't really know what other careers would have the same level of stability and influence like those of doctors. . . . And one where I can feel like I'm making a difference, too.

CAREER COUNSELOR 6: Perhaps we can work in here to explore careers that share some likelihood with a career as a physician, but honor your interests, skills, personal values, and family values, so you don't feel limited to only one career path. [asked in an exploratory manner] I wonder if that would feel useful to you? (Skill 5: Discussing the Benefits of Career Counseling)

CLIENT 6: [*exasperated*] Maybe . . . I just don't even know where to start. I don't know what to do . . . I just know I need to figure this out. I've got to decide on this soon.

CAREER COUNSELOR 7: And deciding on a career path can feel like such a daunting, overwhelming decision. [*in a low, empathic tone*] Before we jump into ideas and next steps, let's pause for a moment and talk a bit about what you've tried so far. What have you done so far to explore alternative career paths? (Skill 3: Exploring Your Client's Decision-Making Styles)

CLIENT 7: Well, I'm taking a few courses this semester outside of my major.

CAREER COUNSELOR 8: That's great! Tell me about the courses. What are the topics and what drew you to them?

CLIENT 8: I'm taking a sociology class and a psychology class this semester. I've thought a bit about being a therapist. I guess I've always been interested in helping people. That's one big reason why I wanted to be a doctor.

CAREER COUNSELOR 9: Yes, I definitely see that connection! It sounds like one thing that might be important for you is to find a career that makes a difference in others' lives—to feel like you are making a meaningful impact. I wonder if aligning with that value might help you feel more excited about some alternative career paths and might spark some excitement for you, even outside of work, in your avocations or hobbies. In thinking about what you would like to do in your spare time or other potential careers, how might you align what you do with your value of helping others? (Skill 2: Exploring Your Client's Values)

CLIENT 9: [*frustrated*] If I knew that, I wouldn't be in here to see you!

CAREER COUNSELOR 10: I understand. Let's try a different question: Tell me about a time when you felt most aligned with the value of helping others. What were you doing, and how might you feel different than you currently feel if your work or hobbies aligned with your value of making a difference and helping others? (Skill 9: Addressing Client Ambivalence and Skepticism)

CLIENT 10: Well, I love to sew. My mother taught me how. We used to sew baby blankets for the premature babies at our local hospital to keep them warm. I've always had a soft spot for children at hospitals, and I found that craft really gratifying.

CAREER COUNSELOR 11: That sounds like such a special memory! Tell me more about what you found most enjoyable about making those blankets for the babies.

CLIENT 11: It felt so satisfying to create something from scratch and to see the impact it made on others. The parents were always so excited to get our handmade creations. I embroidered a special word on each blanket too—like "hope" or "love" or "healthy tomorrows" to encourage the family that received the blanket.

CAREER COUNSELOR 12: What a thoughtful touch! It sounds like you're skilled in creativity and attention to detail too! If those skills are ones you'd like to infuse in a future career, I wonder what potential careers might particularly use creativity, encouragement, and attention to detail. You mentioned you might be interested in being a therapist. How do, or don't, you see that career as aligning with the skills of creativity, encouragement, and attention to detail? (Skill 1: Exploring Your Client's Skills)

CLIENT 12: Umm . . . well, I don't really know much about what being a therapist is really like, so I don't know how to answer that.

CAREER COUNSELOR 13: It's definitely difficult to decide on a career path without much knowledge of the careers in the first place. Perhaps after we spend some more time exploring your values, interests, and skills, we can then begin exploring different career options, and we can also talk through some resources and avenues to explore those careers further. How does that sound? (Skill 6: Setting Session Goals)

CLIENT 13: Yeah, that sounds good.

CAREER COUNSELOR 14: We've talked a bit about some of your family's values—finding a stable career that has some prestige, and we've talked about some of your personal values—finding a career that makes a difference in the lives of others. We've also talked about a few of your skills—creativity, attention to detail, encouraging others. Let's dig in a bit more and talk about some of your other skills. If your best friend was to describe you, what would they say?

CLIENT 14: [*sheepishly*] Hmmm . . . I don't know . . . I guess they'd say I'm kind? I don't know what else they'd say.

CAREER COUNSELOR 15: Okay, yes, this is a good start. Now, let's shift our focus to any previous jobs or volunteer roles you've held, if any. What would your colleagues say about you?

CLIENT 15: Hmm . . . well, they'd say I'm dependable and conscientious—I rarely missed a day of work. I'm a team player. I don't know . . . I don't like talking about myself. It feels like bragging.

CAREER COUNSELOR 16: I get it—it can feel awkward to talk about ourselves. You mentioned that finding a career that gives back to others is important to you. Let's pause for a moment and reflect. When you think back to your last job, tell me about a time when you felt you were helping others.

CLIENT 16: Okay, let me think . . . I used to organize a "Mindfulness Monday" event for my office. Each Monday I would share a new mindfulness practice with them to start the week off in a more thoughtful and present-focused headspace.

CAREER COUNSELOR 17: That sounds really neat—I love the creativity and initiative you took in developing those! Aside from potentially pursuing a career in medicine or therapy, what other careers do you think might capitalize on your creative side? (Skill 1: Exploring Your Client's Skills)

CLIENT 17: Well, I love creating all types of art—that's really creative. I just don't know how I could make a career from that.

CAREER COUNSELOR 18: Yes, I have a few resources that I'll share with you at the end of our session today, which I believe will create a really useful starting point for exploring career options. Before we get there, how would you feel about us spending a bit more time exploring your values, interests, and skills? (Skill 6: Setting Session Goals)

CLIENT 18: Yeah, okay, but I don't really know what else to say about my values, interests, and skills. That's why I'm here—I'm hoping to learn more about myself, so I can make an informed decision on my career path.

CAREER COUNSELOR 19: I get that. It sounds like you're feeling a bit of a block—you'd like to learn more about yourself, but you're not sure what else to say. I wonder if the career assessments you took yesterday might highlight a few things that perhaps you haven't thought about yet or affirm some things you innately know about yourself.

CLIENT 19: Yeah, maybe.

CAREER COUNSELOR 20: The three assessments you took yesterday were designed to explore some of your primary interests, personal values, and skills. One of the things I found really interesting when looking at your assessment results was that they seem to suggest, as you've shared in here, that you have a passion and skill in the areas of creativity and self-expression. The assessments also suggest that you like a good challenge and care deeply for others; you're compassionate and caring. Now, it's important to note at the outset that these assessments may suggest areas of interest, values, and skills, but ultimately, what matters is whether these results seem to resonate with you. We'll talk about some more of the results in a moment, but let's pause first. What is your reaction to hearing these initial assessment results? We've talked a bit about your care for others and your creative side, but the results also suggest you might get bored in a monotonous work environment and crave a good challenge—I'm curious if that resonates with you? (Skill 7: Feedback on Career Assessments)

CLIENT 20: It does. The reason why I didn't like my last job was because I never really felt challenged. I think that's one reason why I created the Mindfulness Monday sessions: to contribute creatively and to push myself to learn about new mindfulness techniques. I think I would get bored in a repetitive job.

CAREER COUNSELOR 21: Okay, so it sounds like you'd thrive in a work environment where each day is a little different—your roles are varied, you're learning new things.

CLIENT 21: Yes! I want to feel engaged at work. I don't want to do the same thing over and over again.

CAREER COUNSELOR 22: Great—okay, so I'm hearing that an ideal career path for you would be one that involves creativity, a variety in your roles at work, opportunities to contribute to the betterment of others, and stability. Now, keeping in mind that these are only suggestions of areas of interest, one other interesting thing I noticed when I was looking at your results was that they seem to suggest that a career involving both innovation and problem solving might be a good fit. What are your thoughts about that? (Skill 8: Exploring Underlying Themes in Assessments)

CLIENT 22: I never really thought about my problem-solving skills before, but I guess I do like to find creative ways to help others. I think that's one reason why I've considered being a therapist—maybe even an art therapist? That might be a creative career. But I don't know anything about therapy, really. How would I even decide on a career without knowing much about it?

CAREER COUNSELOR 23: That's a good question—you mentioned earlier that you've been taking new classes to explore other potential majors or interests. That sounds like an excellent way to get exposure to potential future career paths! What are some other ways you could get exposure to learning more about art therapy, since you mentioned that one, or other related careers?

CLIENT 23: I don't really know what else to do. Maybe I could talk with an art therapist? But I don't even know how to go about that—where would I even find one?

CAREER COUNSELOR 24: I wonder if a first step could be just doing a little research on that career path online. There are a number of free resources online, and the *Occupational Outlook Handbook* (U.S. Bureau of Labor Statistics, 2024) might be a good place to start. You can use their search bar on their website to search "art therapist" or "psychologist" or "counselor," and you'll find a summary on the career, what they do, their work environment, how to become one, the salary you could expect, even the job outlook, which might give you some guidance on the projected stability or growth of that career and similar occupations. What are your thoughts about starting there? (Skill 10: Assigning Homework in Career Counseling)

CLIENT 24: Yeah, I think I could do that.

CAREER COUNSELOR 25: Great! Why don't you do a little digging on that career and perhaps similar occupations listed on the website, and let's meet next week to explore your reactions to what you found and next steps? How does that sound? (Skill 6: Setting Session Goals)

CLIENT 25: Sounds good. I'll see you then!

EXERCISE 12

Mock Career Counseling Sessions

In contrast to highly structured and repetitive deliberate practice exercises, a mock career counseling session is an unstructured and improvised role-play career counseling session. Like a jazz rehearsal, mock sessions let you practice the art and science of *appropriate responsiveness* (Hatcher, 2015; Stiles & Horvath, 2017), putting your career counseling skills together in a way that is helpful to your mock client. This exercise outlines the procedure for conducting a mock career counseling session. It offers different client profiles you may choose to adopt when role-playing the client.

Mock sessions are an opportunity for trainees to practice the following:

- using counseling skills responsively;
- navigating challenging choice points in career counseling;
- choosing which interventions to use;
- tracking the arc of a career counseling session and the overall big-picture career counseling process or intervention;
- guiding treatment in the context of the client's preferences;
- determining realistic goals for career counseling in the context of the client's capacities;
- knowing how to proceed when the career counselor is unsure, lost, or confused;
- recognizing and recovering from counseling errors;
- discovering your personal career counseling style; and
- building endurance for working with real clients.

Mock Career Counseling Session Overview

For the mock session, **you will perform a role-play of an initial career counseling session.** As is true with the exercises to build individual skills, the role-play involves three people: One trainee role-plays the career counselor, another trainee role-plays the client, and a trainer (a professor or a supervisor) observes and provides feedback. This is an open-ended role-play, as is commonly done in training. However, this differs in two important

https://doi.org/10.1037/0000442-014
Deliberate Practice in Career Counseling, by J. M. Taylor, A. Vaz, and T. Rousmaniere
Copyright © 2025 by the American Psychological Association. All rights reserved.

ways from the role-plays used in more traditional training. First, the career counselor will use their hand to indicate how difficult the role-play feels. Second, the client will attempt to make the role-play easier or harder to ensure the career counselor is practicing at the right difficulty level.

Preparation

1. Download the Deliberate Practice Reaction Form and Deliberate Practice Diary Form at https://www.apa.org/pubs/books/deliberate-practice-career-counseling (see the "Resources" tab; also available in Appendixes A and B, respectively). Every student will need their own copy of the Deliberate Practice Reaction Form on a separate piece of paper so they can access it quickly.

2. Designate one student to role-play the career counselor and one student to role-play the client. The trainer will observe and provide corrective feedback.

Mock Career Counseling Session Procedure

1. The trainees will role-play an initial (first) career counseling session. The trainee role-playing the client selects a client profile from the end of this exercise.

2. Before beginning the role-play, the career counselor raises their hand to their side, at the level of their chair seat (see Figure E12.1). They will use this hand throughout the whole role-play to indicate how challenging it feels to them to help the client. Their starting hand level (chair seat) indicates that the role-play feels easy. By raising

FIGURE E12.1. Ongoing Difficulty Assessment Through Hand Level

Note. Left: Start of role-play. Right: Role-play is too difficult. From *Deliberate Practice in Emotion-Focused Therapy* (p. 156), by R. N. Goldman, A. Vaz, and T. Rousmaniere, 2021, American Psychological Association (https://doi.org/10.1037/0000227-000). Copyright 2021 by the American Psychological Association.

their hand, the career counselor indicates that the difficulty is rising. If their hand rises above their neck level, it indicates that the role-play is too difficult.

3. The career counselor begins the role-play. The career counselor and client should engage in the role-play in an improvised manner, as they would engage in a real career counseling session. The career counselor keeps their hand out at their side throughout this process. (This may feel strange at first!)

4. Whenever the career counselor feels that the difficulty of the role-play has changed significantly, they should move their hand up if it feels more difficult, down if it feels easier. If the career counselor's hand drops below the seat of their chair, the client should make the role-play more challenging; if the career counselor's hand rises above their neck level, the client should make the role-play easier. Instructions for adjusting the difficulty of the role-play are described in the Varying the Level of Challenge section.

> **Note to Career Counselors**
>
> Remember to be aware of your vocal quality. Match your tone to the client's presentation. Thus, if the client presents vulnerable, soft emotions behind their words, soften your tone to be soothing and calm. If you choose responses that are prompting client exploration, such as exploring their skills, values, or cultural and familial influences, remember to adopt a more querying, exploratory tone of voice.

5. The role-play continues for at least 15 minutes. The trainer may provide corrective feedback during this process if the career counselor gets significantly off track. However, trainers should exercise restraint and keep feedback as short and tight as possible, as this will reduce the career counselor's opportunity for experiential training.

6. After the role-play is finished, the career counselor and client switch roles and begin a new mock session.

7. After both trainees have completed the mock session as a career counselor, the trainees and the trainer discuss the experience.

Varying the Level of Challenge

If the career counselor indicates that the mock session is too easy, the person enacting the role of the client can use the following modifications to make it more challenging (see also Appendix A):

- The client can improvise with topics that are more evocative or make the career counselor uncomfortable, such as expressing currently held strong feelings (see Figure A.2).
- The client can use a distressed voice (e.g., angry, sad, sarcastic) or unpleasant facial expression. This increases the emotional tone.
- Blend complex mixtures of opposing feelings (e.g., hope and despair).
- Become confrontational, questioning the purpose of career counseling or the career counselor's fitness for the role.

If the career counselor indicates that the mock session is too hard:

- The client can be guided by Figure A.2 to
  - present topics that are less evocative,
  - present material on any topic but without expressing feelings, or
  - present material concerning the future or the past or events outside career counseling.
- The client can ask the questions in a soft voice or with a smile. This softens the emotional stimulus.
- The career counselor can take short breaks during the role-play.
- The trainer can expand the "feedback phase" by discussing general interpersonal feedback or how certain skills connect with career counseling theories.

Mock Session Client Profiles

Following are six client profiles for trainees to use during mock sessions, presented in order of difficulty. The choice of client profile may be determined by the trainee playing the career counselor, the trainee playing the client, or assigned by the trainer.

The most important aspect of role-plays is for trainees to convey the emotional tone indicated by the client profile (e.g., "angry" or "sad"). The demographics of the client (e.g., age, gender) and specific content of the client profiles are not essential to this particular training exercise. Thus, trainees should adjust the client profile to be most comfortable and easy for the trainee to role-play. For example, a trainee may change the client profile from female to male, from 45 to 22 years old, and so on.

Beginner Profile: Exploring Interests and Values With an Intuitive and Engaged Client

Maria is a 27-year-old Latina, Christian, heterosexual, cis-woman. She is a nontraditional college student. Maria is returning to college after spending the past decade in a career of waitressing. She enjoys helping others and would like to explore career options that align with her values (leadership, responsibility, trustworthiness, kindness, and service).

- **Presenting challenges:** Deciding on a major and choosing a career path
- **Client's goals for career counseling:** Maria wants to explore potential career options that align with her values, primarily related to helping others and making society a "better place."
- **Attitude toward career counseling:** Maria had good experiences in both personal counseling and with a career advisor when she was in high school and is optimistic that counseling could help her again.
- **Strengths:** Maria is very motivated for career counseling and is emotionally open with the career counselor. She is naturally curious and open-minded and possesses positive self-efficacy and confidence related to her ability to succeed across a range of career options.

Beginner Profile: Supporting a Client Who Is Burned Out in Their Current Career

Arthur is a 25-year-old bisexual, agnostic, nonbinary African American emergency room health care worker who feels burned out in their current career and is considering a career move or finding strategies to make their current career more manageable in the long run. Arthur works a late-night shift; a shift that has felt very isolating. They feel on edge at work and are considering moving to a career that they consider less stressful.

- **Presenting challenges:** Loneliness, stress, and exhaustion
- **Client's goals for career counseling:** Arthur hopes to find better work–life balance and connections with others, either in their current career or by transitioning to a new one.
- **Attitude toward career counseling:** Arthur had positive experiences in career counseling in the past. They are hopeful that this experience will help as well.
- **Strengths:** Arthur is emotionally open and motivated to engage in the career counseling process.

Intermediate Profile: Exploring Strengths and Preparing for Interviews With a Client Who Was Recently Laid Off

Lee is a 67-year-old pansexual atheist cis-man who was laid off from his job as a factory worker 3 weeks ago. He is very hardworking and built many friendships over his 30-year career at the factory. Because of this, he is experiencing significant grief with the loss of his job. He dropped out of high school when he was a sophomore but received his general equivalency diploma (GED) 8 years ago. He worries that age discrimination was the reason he was let go from his job, and he is concerned that others will not hire him because he is an older employee. He has been interviewing for other positions since then, and fortunately, he has secured three job interviews. He wants to give his utmost effort in his interviews and struggles to identify his strengths. He would like support in preparing for his upcoming job interviews, anticipating that he may need to play up his strengths. Lee grew up in an underserved area of the Midwest and was taught from a young age to be humble. Discussing his strengths has been a struggle for him, given the messages he has internalized.

- **Presenting challenges:** Grief related to losing his job, stress related to finding a new job, concerns related to age discrimination, dealing with internalization of his job less, and feelings of failure and rejection
- **Client's goals for career counseling:** Lee wants to feel more confident as he heads into his job interviews and hopes to explore and become more comfortable talking about his strengths.
- **Attitude toward career counseling:** Lee didn't want to come to career counseling, because he felt very nervous about it and thinks that the career counselor will judge him. Lee's partner convinced him to try career counseling.
- **Strengths:** Underneath his shame and doubt, Lee really wants to connect with other people, including the career counselor.

Intermediate Profile: Helping a Sarcastic and Skeptical Client Who Feels Trapped in His Career

Mehmet is a 45-year-old, heterosexual, married, Muslim, Turkish cis-man and software engineer who was encouraged to try out career counseling because his wife, Selen, thought it might be helpful. He recently interviewed for a promotion at work, but the promotion was instead given to someone who started at the company only 3 months ago

(Mehmet has been working in the same position for the past 4 years). Mehmet feels frustrated and unappreciated at work. He worries he may be "stuck" in his same position for the next 4 years as well.

- **Presenting challenges:** Outbursts of sarcasm and meanness that cover feelings of rejection and despair
- **Client's goals for career counseling:** Mehmet wants to feel "unstuck" at work. He wishes his work was more fulfilling and offered more opportunities for advancement and challenge.
- **Attitude toward career counseling:** Mehmet has never been in career counseling before and is skeptical as to whether it will help. He came because his wife asked him to do so, but he's not sure what value career counseling could provide.
- **Strengths:** Mehmet is hardworking and wants to provide financially for his family. Mehmet is not afraid of a challenge.

Advanced Profile: Narrowing Down Career Interests With an Indecisive Client

April is a 58-year-old, first-generation, Buddhist Asian American law school graduate student who has dyslexia. She has many talents and is excelling in all her law school classes. One of her greatest challenges has been narrowing down her area of interest in law school. She often worries about making the wrong decision or making a mistake. She is considering a career in criminal law, family law, or international law. It is also worth noting that April has experienced significant pain and trauma due to systemic racism and discrimination, particularly from some of her classmates who have created a hostile environment for her.

- **Presenting challenges:** Difficulty in decision making, stress related to determining her career path and impending choices for internship applications, stress related to systemic racism, and racist members of her law school cohort
- **Client's goals for career counseling:** As she approaches the internship application process, April aims to refine her career interests and make a well-informed decision regarding her specialization/concentration in law school.
- **Attitude toward career counseling:** April went to career counseling in college but had a bad experience. She said that the sessions lacked direction, and she didn't feel she got much out of the process.
- **Strengths:** April is a bright, ambitious, articulate, motivated law student who is excelling in all her courses. She is extremely hardworking and has overcome many obstacles in the past.

Advanced Profile: Adjusting to a Career Layoff

Gretchen is a 41-year-old Jewish White transgender woman with three young children (aged 3, 5, and 7) whom she adopted last year. She is a single mother and an electrician who was recently laid off from work. She is very stressed with the impact her job layoff is causing on her family, as she struggles to provide for her three children in addition to herself. She has been dealing with the stress by cutting and drinking. She has also dealt with discrimination and biases from others as a result of her gender identity and worries about discrimination she may face as she applies for more jobs.

- **Presenting challenges:** Stress related to job and financial instability, mood lability, and self-harm
- **Client's goals for career counseling:** Gretchen wants support as she finds a new job and hopes career counseling can provide her with concrete suggestions regarding what to do to prepare for a new job. She is also hoping for support related to the stress of unemployment.
- **Attitude toward career counseling:** Although Gretchen has not engaged in career counseling in the past, she has engaged in personal counseling. She found personal counseling helpful until the counselor disappointed Gretchen by transitioning her to another counselor while her counselor was on maternity leave. As a result, Gretchen felt abandoned and did not trust the new counselor. She worries that you may abandon her too. She also worries that she does not have time for career counseling, particularly given how critical it is for her to invest her energy in finding a new job.
- **Strengths:** Gretchen is very open to what the career counselor says (when she feels safe in career counseling). Gretchen is ambitious and resilient and has overcome many setbacks she has faced in the past.

… PART III

Strategies for Enhancing the Deliberate Practice Exercises

Part III consists of one chapter, Chapter 3, that provides additional advice and instructions for trainers and trainees so that they can reap more benefits from the deliberate practice exercises in Part II. Chapter 3 offers six key points for getting the most out of deliberate practice, guidelines for practicing appropriately responsive treatment, evaluation strategies, methods for ensuring trainee well-being and respecting their privacy, and advice for monitoring the trainer–trainee relationship.

How to Get the Most Out of Deliberate Practice: Additional Guidance for Trainers and Trainees

CHAPTER 3

In Chapter 2 and in the exercises themselves, we have provided instructions for completing these deliberate practice exercises. This chapter provides guidance on big-picture topics that trainers will need to successfully integrate deliberate practice into their training program. This guidance is based on relevant research and the experiences and feedback from trainers at more than a dozen mental health training programs who volunteered to test the deliberate practice exercises in this book. We cover topics including evaluation, getting the most from deliberate practice, trainee well-being, respecting trainee privacy, trainer self-evaluation, responsive treatment, and the trainee–trainer alliance.

Six Key Points for Getting the Most From Deliberate Practice

The following are six key points of advice for trainers and trainees to get the most benefit from the career counseling deliberate practice exercises. The advice is gleaned from experiences vetting and practicing the exercises, sometimes in different languages, with many trainees, across many countries.

Key Point 1: Create Realistic Emotional Stimuli

A key component of deliberate practice is using stimuli that provoke similar reactions to challenging real-life work settings. For example, pilots train with flight simulators that present mechanical failures and dangerous weather conditions; surgeons practice with surgical simulators that present medical complications with only seconds to respond. Training with challenging stimuli will increase trainees' capacity to perform career counseling effectively under stress, for example with clients they find challenging. The stimuli used for career counseling deliberate practice exercises are role-plays of challenging client statements in counseling. **It is important that the trainee who is role-playing the client performs the script with appropriate emotional expression and maintains eye contact with the career counselor.** For example, if the client statement

https://doi.org/10.1037/0000442-015
Deliberate Practice in Career Counseling, by J. M. Taylor, A. Vaz, and T. Rousmaniere
Copyright © 2025 by the American Psychological Association. All rights reserved.

calls for sad emotion, the trainee should try to express sadness eye-to-eye with the career counselor. We offer the suggestions regarding emotional expressiveness:

1. The emotional tone of the role-play matters more than the exact words of each script. Trainees role-playing the client should feel free to improvise and change the words if it will help them be more emotionally expressive. Trainees do not need to stick 100% exactly to the script. In fact, to read off the script during the exercise can sound flat and prohibit eye contact. Rather, trainees in the client role should first read the client statement silently to themselves, then, when ready, say it in an emotional manner while looking directly at the trainee playing the career counselor. This will help the experience feel more real and engaging for the career counselor.

2. Trainees whose first language isn't English may particularly benefit from reviewing and changing the words in the client statement script before each role-play so that they can find words that feel congruent and facilitate emotional expression.

3. Trainees role-playing the client should try to use tonal and nonverbal expressions of feelings. For example, if a script calls for anger, the trainee can speak with an angry voice and make fists with their hands; if a script calls for shame or guilt, the trainee could hunch over and wince; if a script calls for sadness, the trainee could speak in a soft or deflated voice.

4. If trainees are having persistent difficulties acting believably when following a particular script in the role of client, it may help to first do a "demo round" by reading directly from paper and then, immediately after, dropping the paper to make eye contact and repeating the same client statement from memory. Some trainees reported this helped them "become available as a real client" and made the role-play feel less artificial. Some trainees did three or four demo rounds to get fully into their role as a client.

Key Point 2: Customize the Exercises to Fit Your Unique Training Circumstances

Deliberate practice is less about adhering to specific rules than it is about using training principles. Every trainer has their own individual teaching style and every trainee their own learning process. Thus, the exercises in this book are designed to be flexibly customized by trainers across different training contexts within different cultures. Trainees and trainers are encouraged to adjust exercises continually to optimize their practice. The most effective training will occur when deliberate practice exercises are customized to fit the learning needs of each trainee and culture of each training site. In our experience with numerous trainers and trainees across many countries, we found that everyone spontaneously customized the exercises for their unique training circumstances. No two trainers followed the exact same procedure. For example:

- One supervisor used the exercises with a trainee who found all the client statements to be too hard, including the "beginner" stimuli. This trainee had multiple reactions in the "too hard" category, including nausea, severe shame, and self-doubt. The trainee disclosed to the supervisor that she had experienced extremely harsh learning environments earlier in her life and found the role-plays to be highly evocative. To help, the supervisor followed the suggestions offered in Appendix A to make the stimuli progressively easier until the trainee reported feeling "good challenge" on the Deliberate Practice Reaction Form. Over many weeks of practice, the trainee developed a sense of safety and was able to practice with more difficult client statements. (Note that if the supervisor had proceeded at the too hard difficulty level, the trainee might have complied while hiding her negative reactions, becoming emotionally flooded and overwhelmed, leading to withdrawal and thus prohibiting her skill development and risking dropout from training.)

- Supervisors of trainees for whom English was not their first language adjusted the client statements to their own primary language.

- One supervisor used the exercises with a trainee who found all the stimuli to be too easy, including the advanced client statements. This supervisor quickly moved to improvising more challenging client statements from scratch by following the instructions in Appendix A on how to make client statements more challenging.

Key Point 3: Discover Your Own Unique Personal Career Counseling Style

Deliberate practice in career counseling can be likened to the process of learning to play jazz music. Every jazz musician prides themselves in their skillful improvisations, and the process of "finding your own voice" is a prerequisite for expertise in jazz musicianship. Yet improvisations are not a collection of random notes but the culmination of extensive deliberate practice over time. Indeed, the ability to improvise is built on many hours of dedicated practice of scales, melodies, harmonies, and so on. Much in the same way, career counseling trainees are encouraged to experience the scripted interventions in this book not as ends in themselves but as a means to promote skill in a systematic fashion. Over time, effective career counseling creativity can be aided, instead of constrained, by dedicated practice in these counseling "melodies."

Key Point 4: Engage in a Sufficient Amount of Rehearsal

Deliberate practice uses rehearsal to move skills into procedural memory, which helps trainees maintain access to skills even when working with challenging clients. This only works if trainees engage in many repetitions of the exercises. Think of a challenging sport or musical instrument you learned: How many rehearsals would a professional need to feel confident performing a new skill? Career counseling is no easier than those other fields!

Key Point 5: Continually Adjust Difficulty

A crucial element of deliberate practice is training at an optimal difficulty level: neither too easy nor too hard. To achieve this, do difficulty assessments and adjustments with the Deliberate Practice Reaction Form in Appendix A. **Do not skip this step!** If trainees don't feel any of the "good challenge" reactions at the bottom of the Deliberate Practice Reaction Form, then the exercise is probably too easy; if they feel any of the "too hard" reactions then the exercise could be too difficult for the trainee to benefit. Advanced trainees and counselors may find all the client statements too easy. If so, they should follow the instructions in Appendix A on making client statements harder to make the role-plays sufficiently challenging.

Key Point 6: Putting It All Together With the Practice Transcript and Mock Career Counseling Sessions

Some trainees may seek greater contextualization of the individual career counseling responses associated with each skill, feeling the need to integrate the disparate pieces of their training in a more coherent manner with a simulation that mimics a real career counseling session. The annotated transcript in Exercise 11 and the mock career counseling sessions in Exercise 12 give trainees this opportunity, allowing them to practice delivering different responses sequentially in a more realistic career counseling encounter.

Responsive Treatment

The exercises in this book are designed not only to help trainees acquire specific skills of career counseling, but to use them in ways that are responsive to each individual client. Across the counseling and psychotherapy literature, this stance has been referred to as *appropriate responsiveness*, wherein the counselors exercise flexible judgment, based in their perception of the client's emotional state, needs, and goals, and integrates techniques and other interpersonal skills in pursuit of optimal client outcomes (Hatcher, 2015; Stiles et al., 1998). The effective counselor or therapist is responsive to the emerging context. As Stiles and Horvath (2017) argued, they are effective because they are appropriately responsive. Doing the "right thing" may be different each time and means providing each client with an individually tailored response.

Appropriate responsiveness counters a misconception that deliberate practice rehearsal is designed to promote robotic repetition of counseling and therapy techniques. Psychotherapy researchers have shown that over-adherence to a particular model while neglecting client preferences reduces therapy effectiveness (e.g., Castonguay et al., 1996; Henry et al., 1993; Owen & Hilsenroth, 2014). Counselor/therapist flexibility, on the other hand, has been shown to improve outcomes (e.g., Bugatti & Boswell, 2016; Kendall & Beidas, 2007; Kendall & Frank, 2018). It is important, therefore, that trainees practice their newly learned skills in a manner that is flexible and responsive to the unique needs of a diverse range of clients (Hatcher, 2015; Hill & Knox, 2013). It is thus of paramount importance for trainees to develop the necessary perceptual skills to be able to attune to what the client is experiencing in the moment and form their response based on the client moment-by-moment context (Greenberg & Goldman, 1988).

Supervisors must help the supervisee to specifically attune themselves to the unique and specific needs of the clients during sessions. By enacting responsiveness with the supervisee, the supervisor can demonstrate its value and make it more explicit. In these ways, attention can be given to the larger picture of appropriate responsiveness. Here the trainee and supervisor can work together to help the trainee master not just the techniques but also how the career counselor can use their judgment to put the techniques together to foster positive change. Helping trainees keep this overarching goal in mind while reviewing the counseling process is a valuable feature of supervision that is difficult to obtain otherwise (Hatcher, 2015).

It is also important that deliberate practice occurs within a context of wider career counseling learning. As noted in Chapter 1, training should be combined with supervision of actual career counseling recordings, theoretical learning, observation of competent career counseling approaches, as well as personal counseling work. When the trainer or trainee determines that the trainee is having difficulty acquiring particular career counseling skills, it is important to carefully assess what is missing or needed. Assessment should then lead to the appropriate remedy, as the trainer and trainee collaboratively determine what is needed.

Being Mindful of Trainee Well-Being

Although negative effects that some clients experience in counseling and psychotherapy have been well documented (Barlow, 2010), negative effects of training and supervision on trainees have received less attention (Ellis et al., 2014). Research on effective career counseling supervision does suggest, however, that attending to the working alliance between the supervisor and supervisee early in the supervision process, acknowledging the power differentials between trainers and trainees, and attuning to affect in supervision are all critical to supporting effective career counseling training and supervision (Parcover & Swanson, 2013).

To support strong self-efficacy, trainers must ensure that trainees are practicing at a correct difficulty level. The exercises in this book feature guidance for frequently assessing and adjusting the difficulty level, so that trainees can rehearse at a level that precisely targets their personal skill threshold. Trainers and supervisors must be mindful to provide an appropriate challenge. One risk to trainees that is particularly pertinent to this book occurs when using role-plays that are too difficult. The Deliberate Practice Reaction Form in Appendix A is provided to help trainers ensure that role-plays are done at an appropriate challenge level. Trainers or trainees may be tempted to skip the difficulty assessments and adjustments, out of their motivation to focus on rehearsal to make fast progress and quickly acquire skills. But across all our test sites, we found that skipping the difficulty assessments and adjustments caused more problems and hindered skill acquisition more than any other error. Thus, trainers are advised to remember that **one of their most important responsibilities is to remind trainees to do the difficulty assessments and adjustments.**

Additionally, the Deliberate Practice Reaction Form serves a dual purpose of helping trainees develop the important skills of self-monitoring and self-awareness (Bennett-Levy, 2019). This will help trainees adopt a positive and empowered stance regarding their own self-care and should facilitate career-long professional development.

Respecting Trainee Privacy

The deliberate practice exercises in this book may stir up complex or uncomfortable personal reactions within trainees, including for example memories of past traumas. Exploring psychological and emotional reactions may make some trainees feel vulnerable. Career counselors of every career stage, from trainees to seasoned career counselors with decades of experience, commonly experience shame, embarrassment, and self-doubt in this process. Although these experiences can be valuable for building trainees' self-awareness, it is important that training remains focused on professional skill development and not blur into personal therapy (e.g., Ellis et al., 2014). Therefore, one trainer role is to remind trainees to maintain appropriate boundaries.

Trainees must have the final say about what to disclose or not disclose to their trainer. Trainees should keep in mind that the goal is for the trainee to expand their own self-awareness and psychological capacity to stay active and helpful while experiencing uncomfortable reactions. The trainer does not need to know the specific details about the trainee's inner world for this to happen.

Trainees should be instructed to share only personal information that they feel comfortable sharing. The Deliberate Practice Reaction Form and difficulty assessment process is designed to help trainees build their self-awareness while retaining control over their privacy. Trainees can be reminded that the goal is for them to learn about their own inner world. They do not necessarily have to share that information with trainers or peers (Bennett-Levy & Finlay-Jones, 2018). Likewise, trainees should be instructed to respect the confidentiality of their peers.

Trainer Self-Evaluation

The exercises in this book were tested at a wide range of training sites around the world, including graduate courses, practicum sites, and private practice offices. Although trainers reported that the exercises were highly effective for training, some also said that they felt disoriented by how different deliberate practice feels when compared with their traditional methods of clinical education. Many felt comfortable evaluating their trainees' performance but were less sure about their own performance as trainers.

The most common concern we heard from trainers was, "My trainees are doing great, but I'm not sure if I am doing this correctly!" To address this concern, we recommend trainers perform periodic self-evaluations along the following five criteria:

1. Observe the trainee's work performance.
2. Provide continual corrective feedback.
3. Ensure rehearsal of specific skills is just beyond the trainee's current ability.
4. Ensure that the trainee is practicing at the right difficulty level (neither too easy nor too challenging).
5. Continuously assess trainee performance with real clients.

Criterion 1: Observe the Trainee's Work Performance

Determining how well we are doing as trainers means first having valid information about how well trainees are responding to training. This requires that we directly observe trainees practicing skills to provide corrective feedback and evaluation. One risk of deliberate practice is that trainees gain competence in performing career counseling skills in role-plays, but those skills do not transfer to trainees' work with real clients. Thus, trainers will ideally also have the opportunity to observe samples of trainees' work with real clients, either live or via recorded video. Supervisors and consultants rely heavily—and, too often, exclusively—on supervisees' and consultees' narrative accounts of their work with clients (Goodyear & Nelson, 1997). Haggerty and Hilsenroth (2011) described this challenge:

> Suppose a loved one has to undergo surgery and you need to choose between two surgeons, one of whom has never been directly observed by an experienced surgeon while performing any surgery. He or she would perform the surgery and return to his or her attending physician and try to recall, sometimes incompletely or inaccurately, the intricate steps of the surgery they just performed. It is hard to imagine that anyone, given a choice, would prefer this over a professional who has been routinely observed in the practice of their craft. (p. 193)

Criterion 2: Provide Continual Corrective Feedback

Trainees need corrective feedback to learn what they are doing well, doing poorly, and how to improve their skills. Feedback should be as specific and incremental as possible. The following are examples of specific feedback: "Your voice sounds rushed. Try slowing down by pausing for a few seconds between your statements to the client," and "That's excellent how you are making eye contact with the client." Examples of vague and nonspecific feedback are, "Try to build better rapport with the client," and "Try to be more open to the client's feelings."

Criterion 3: Specific Skill Rehearsal Just Beyond the Trainee's Current Ability (Zone of Proximal Development)

Deliberate practice emphasizes skill acquisition via behavioral rehearsal. Trainers should endeavor not to get caught up in client conceptualization at the expense of focusing on skills. For many trainers, this requires significant discipline and self-restraint. It is simply more enjoyable to talk about career counseling theory (e.g., case conceptualization, treatment planning, nuances of career counseling models, similar cases the supervisor has had) than watch trainees rehearse skills. Trainees have many questions, and supervisors have an abundance of experience; the allotted supervision time can easily be filled sharing knowledge. The supervisor gets to sound smart, while the trainee doesn't have to struggle with acquiring skills at their learning edge. Although answering questions is important, trainees' intellectual knowledge about career counseling can quickly surpass their procedural ability to perform career counseling, particularly with clients they find challenging. Here's a simple rule of thumb: The trainer provides the knowledge, but the behavioral rehearsal provides the skill (Rousmaniere, 2019).

Criterion 4: Practice at the Right Difficulty Level (Neither Too Easy nor Too Challenging)

Deliberate practice involves *optimal strain*: practicing skills just beyond the trainee's current skill threshold so that they can learn incrementally without becoming overwhelmed (Ericsson, 2006).

Trainers should use difficulty assessments and adjustments throughout deliberate practice to ensure that trainees are practicing at the right difficulty level. Note that some trainees are surprised by their unpleasant reactions to exercises (e.g., dissociation, nausea, blanking out), and may be tempted to "push through" exercises that are too hard. This can happen out of fear of failing a course, fear of being judged as incompetent, or negative self-impressions by the trainee (e.g., "This shouldn't be so hard"). Trainers should normalize the fact that there will be wide variation in perceived difficulty of the exercises and encourage trainees to respect their own personal training process.

Criterion 5: Continuously Assess Trainee Performance With Real Clients

The goal of deliberately practicing career counseling skills is to improve trainees' effectiveness at helping real clients. One of the risks in deliberate practice training is that the benefits will not generalize: Trainees' acquired competence in specific skills may not translate into work with real clients. Thus, it is important that trainers assess the impact of deliberate practice on trainees' work with real clients. Ideally, this is done through triangulation of multiple data points:

- Client data (verbal self-report and routine outcome monitoring data)
- Supervisor's report
- Trainee's self-report

If the trainee's effectiveness with real clients is not improving after deliberate practice, the trainer should do a careful assessment of the difficulty. If the supervisor or trainer feels it is a skill acquisition issue, they may want to consider adjusting the deliberate practice routine to better suit the trainee's learning needs or style.

Counselors have traditionally been evaluated from a lens of *process accountability* (Markman & Tetlock, 2000; see also Goodyear, 2015), which focuses on demonstrating specific behaviors (e.g., fidelity to a treatment model) without regard to the impact on clients. We propose that clinical effectiveness is better assessed through a lens tightly focused on client outcomes and that learning objectives shift from performing behaviors that experts have decided are effective (i.e., the competence model) to highly individualized behavioral goals tailored to each trainee's zone of proximal development and performance feedback. This model of assessment has been termed *outcome accountability*

(Goodyear, 2015), which focuses on client changes, rather than counselor competence, independent of how the counselor might be performing expected tasks.

Guidance for Trainees

The central theme of this book has been that skill rehearsal is not automatically helpful. Deliberate practice must be done well for trainees to benefit (Ericsson & Pool, 2016). In this chapter and in the exercises, we offer guidance for effective deliberate practice. We would also like to provide additional advice specifically for trainees. That advice is drawn from what we have learned at our volunteer deliberate practice test-sites around the world. We cover how to discover your own training process, active effort, playfulness and taking breaks during deliberate practice, your right to control your self-disclosure to trainers, monitoring training results, monitoring complex reactions toward the trainer, and your own personal therapy.

Individualized Career Counseling Training: Finding Your Zone of Proximal Development

Deliberate practice works best when training targets each trainee's personal skill thresholds. Also termed the *zone of proximal development*, a term first coined by Vygotsky in reference to developmental learning theory (Zaretskii, 2009), this is the area just beyond the trainee's current ability but that is possible to reach with the assistance of a teacher or coach (Wass & Golding, 2014). **If a deliberate practice exercise is either too easy or too hard, the trainee will not benefit.** To maximize training productivity, elite performers follow a "challenging but not overwhelming" principle: Tasks that are too far beyond their capacity will prove ineffective and even harmful, but it is equally true that mindlessly repeating what they can already do confidently will prove fruitless. Because of this, deliberate practice requires ongoing assessment of the trainee's current skill and concurrent difficulty adjustment to target a "good enough" challenge consistently. Thus, if you are practicing Exercise 8, "Exploring Underlying Themes in Assessments," and it just feels too difficult, consider moving back to a more comfortable skill such as Exercise 7, "Feedback on Career Assessments," or Exercise 3, "Exploring Your Client's Decision-Making Styles," which they may feel they have already mastered.

Active Effort

It is important for trainees to maintain an active and sustained effort while doing the deliberate practice exercises in this book. Deliberate practice really helps when trainees push themselves up to and past their current ability. This is best achieved when trainees take ownership of their own practice by guiding their training partners to adjust role-plays to be as high on the difficulty scale as possible without hurting themselves. This will look different for every trainee. Although it can feel uncomfortable or even frightening, this is the zone of proximal development where the most gains can be made. Simply reading and repeating the written scripts will provide little or no benefit. Trainees are advised to remember that their effort from training should lead to more confidence and comfort in session with real clients.

Stay the Course: Effort Versus Flow

Deliberate practice only works if trainees push themselves hard enough to break out of their old patterns of performance, which then permits growth of new skills (Ericsson &

Pool, 2016). Because deliberate practice constantly focuses on the current edge of one's performance capacity, it is inevitably a straining endeavor. Indeed, professionals are unlikely to make lasting performance improvements unless there is sufficient engagement in tasks that are just at the edge of one's current capacity (Ericsson, 2003, 2006). From athletics or fitness training, many of us are familiar with this process of being pushed out of our comfort zones followed by adaptation. The same process applies to our mental and emotional abilities.

Many trainees might be surprised to discover that deliberate practice for career counseling feels harder than career counseling with a real client. This may be because when working with a real client a career counselor can get into a state of *flow* (Csikszentmihalyi, 1997), where work feels effortless. In such cases, career counselors may want to move back to offering response formats with which they are more familiar and feel more proficient and try those for a short time, in part to increase a sense of confidence and mastery.

Discover Your Own Training Process

The effectiveness of deliberate practice is directly related to the effort and ownership trainees exert while doing the exercises. Trainers can provide guidance, but it is important for trainees to learn about their own idiosyncratic training processes over time. This will let them become masters of their own training and prepare for a career-long process of professional development. The following are a few examples of personal training processes trainees discovered while engaging in deliberate practice:

- One trainee noticed that she was good at persisting when an exercise was challenging, but that she required more rehearsal than other trainees to feel comfortable with a new skill. This trainee focused on developing patience with her own pace of progress.

- One trainee noticed that he could acquire new skills rather quickly, with only a few repetitions. However, he also noticed that his reactions to evocative client statements could jump very quickly and unpredictably from the "good challenge" to "too hard" categories, so he needed to attend carefully to the reactions listed in the Deliberate Practice Reaction Form.

- One trainee described themself as "perfectionistic" and felt a strong urge to "push through" an exercise even when they had anxiety reactions in the "too hard" category, such as nausea and dissociation. This caused the trainee not to benefit from the exercises and risk getting demoralized. This trainee focused on going slower, developing self-compassion regarding their anxiety reactions, and asking their training partners to make role-plays less challenging.

Trainees are encouraged to reflect deeply on their own experiences using the exercises to learn the most about themselves and their personal learning processes.

Playfulness and Taking Breaks

Career counseling is serious work that can involve painful feelings. However, practicing counseling can be playful and fun (Scott Miller, personal communication, 2017). Trainees should remember that one of the main goals of deliberate practice is to experiment with different approaches and styles of career counseling. If deliberate practice ever feels rote, boring, or routine, it probably isn't going to help advance trainees' skill. In this case, trainees should try to liven it up. A good way to do this is to introduce an atmosphere of playfulness. For example, trainees can try the following:

- Use different vocal tones, speech pacing, body gestures, or other languages. This can expand trainees' communication range.
- Practice while simulating being blind (with a blindfold). This can increase sensitivity of the other senses.
- Practice while standing up or walking around outside. This can help trainees get new perspectives on the process of career counseling.

The supervisor can also ask trainees if they would like to take a 5- to 10-minute break between questions, particularly if they are dealing with difficult emotions and are feeling stressed.

Additional Deliberate Practice Opportunities

This book focuses on deliberate practice methods that involve active, live engagement between trainees and a supervisor. Importantly, deliberate practice can extend beyond these focused training sessions and can be used for homework. For example, a trainee might read the client stimuli quietly or aloud and practice their responses independently between sessions with a supervisor. In such cases, it is important for the trainee to say their career counselor responses aloud, rather than rehearse silently in one's head. Alternatively, two trainees can practice as a pair, without the supervisor. Although the absence of a supervisor limits one source of feedback, the peer trainee who is playing the client can serve this role, as they can when a supervisor is present.

To optimize the quality of the deliberate practice when conducted independently or without a supervisor, we have developed a Deliberate Practice Diary Form that can be found in Appendix B or downloaded from https://www.apa.org/pubs/books/deliberate-practice-career-counseling (see the "Resources" tab). This form provides a template for the trainee to record their experience of the deliberate practice activity, and, ideally, it will aid in the consolidation of learning. This form can be used as part of the evaluation process with the supervisor but is not necessarily intended for that purpose, and trainees are certainly welcome to bring their experience with the independent practice into the next meeting with the supervisor.

Monitoring Training Results

While trainers will evaluate trainees using a competency-focused model, trainees are also encouraged to take ownership of their own training process and look for results of deliberate practice themselves. Trainees should experience the results of deliberate practice within a few training sessions. A lack of results can be demoralizing for trainees and can result in trainees applying less effort and focus in deliberate practice. Trainees who are not seeing results should openly discuss this problem with their trainer and experiment with adjusting their deliberate practice process. Results can include client outcomes and improving the trainee's own work as a career counselor, their personal development, and their overall training.

Client Outcomes

The most important result of deliberate practice is an improvement in trainees' client outcomes. This can be assessed via routine outcome measurement (Lambert, 2010;

Prescott et al., 2017), qualitative data (McLeod, 2017), and informal discussions with clients. However, trainees should note that an improvement in client outcome due to deliberate practice can sometimes be challenging to achieve quickly, given that the largest amount of variance in client outcomes is due to client variables (Bohart & Wade, 2013). For example, a client with severe chronic concerns may not respond quickly to any intervention, regardless of how effectively a trainee practices. For some clients, an increase in patience and self-compassion regarding their concerns may be a sign of progress, rather than an immediate decrease in concerns. Thus, trainees are advised to keep their expectations for client change realistic in the context of their client's concerns, history, and presentation. It is important that trainees do not try to force their clients to improve in counseling so that the trainee feels like they are making progress in their training (Rousmaniere, 2016).

Trainee's Work as a Career Counselor

One important result of deliberate practice is change within the trainee regarding their work with clients. For example, trainees at test sites reported feeling more comfortable sitting with evocative clients, more confident addressing uncomfortable topics in counseling, and more responsive to a broader range of clients.

Trainee's Personal Development

Another important result of deliberate practice is personal growth of the trainee. For example, trainees at test sites reported becoming more in touch with their own feelings and gaining increased self-compassion and enhanced motivation to work with a broader range of clients.

Trainee's Training Process

Another valuable result of deliberate practice is improvement in the trainees' training process. For example, trainees at test sites reported becoming more aware of their personal training style, preferences, strengths, and challenges. Over time, trainees should grow to feel more ownership of their training process. Also, training to be a career counselor is a complex process that occurs over many years. Experienced, expert mental health professionals still report continuing to grow well beyond their graduate school years (Orlinsky & Ronnestad, 2005). Becoming a certified career counselor through the National Career Development Association, for example, requires extensive supervised clinical experience and training. Furthermore, training is not a linear process. As mentioned earlier, some exercises may seem easier, and others may appear more challenging. Some may evoke certain emotions or trigger memories of career struggles experienced by you, your family, and/or loved ones. Some days you may feel more focused and attuned to your mock clients than others. It is common to get caught up in our thoughts, but remember to be gentle with yourself. The exercises in this book are designed to be challenging yet achievable; this is where you will experience the most significant personal and professional growth.

The Trainee–Trainer Alliance: Monitoring Complex Reactions Toward the Trainer

Trainees who engage in difficult deliberate practice often report experiencing complex feelings toward their trainer. For example, one trainee said, "I know this is helping, but I also don't look forward to it!" Another trainee reported feeling both appreciation and frustration toward her trainer simultaneously. Trainees are advised to remember intensive training they have done in other fields, such as athletics or music. When a coach pushes a trainee to the edge of their ability, it is common for trainees to have complex reactions toward that person.

This does not necessarily mean that the trainer is doing anything wrong. In fact, intensive training inevitably stirs up reactions toward the trainer, such as frustration, annoyance, disappointment, or anger that coexist with the appreciations they feel. In fact, if trainees do not experience complex reactions, it is worth considering whether the deliberate practice is sufficiently challenging. But what we asserted earlier about rights to privacy apply here as well. Because professional mental health training is hierarchical, and evaluative, trainers should not require nor even expect trainees to share complex reactions they may be experiencing toward them. Trainers should stay open to their sharing, but the choice always remains with the trainee.

Trainee's Own Therapy

When engaging in deliberate practice, many trainees discover aspects of their inner world that may benefit from attending their own psychotherapy. For example, one trainee discovered that her clients' anger stirred up her own painful memories of abuse, another trainee found himself disassociating while practicing empathy skills, and another trainee experienced overwhelming shame and self-judgment when they couldn't master skills after just a few repetitions.

Although these discoveries were unnerving at first, they were ultimately very beneficial because they motivated the trainees to seek out their own therapy. Many therapists and counselors attend their own therapy. In fact, Norcross and Guy (2005) found in their review of 17 studies that about 75% of the more than 8,000 therapist participants have attended their own therapy. Orlinsky and Ronnestad (2005) found that more than 90% of therapists who attended their own therapy reported it to be helpful. Edwards (2018) employed the Critical Interpretive Synthesis method and discovered that although beginning therapy can be difficult for some trainees, engaging in personal therapy offers a range of benefits, including gaining insights that can be applied to professional clinical practice, ongoing personal growth, and enhanced learning throughout a student's training journey.

QUESTIONS FOR TRAINEES

1. Are you balancing the effort to improve your skills with patience and self-compassion for your learning process?
2. Are you attending to any shame or self-judgment arising from training?
3. Are you being mindful of your personal boundaries and also respecting any complex feelings you may have toward your trainers?

APPENDIX A

Difficulty Assessments and Adjustments

Deliberate practice works best if the exercises are performed at a good challenge that is neither too hard nor too easy. To ensure that they are practicing at the correct difficulty, trainees should do a difficulty assessment and adjustment after each level of client statement is completed (beginner, intermediate, and advanced). To do this, use the following instructions and the Deliberate Practice Reaction Form (Figure A.1), which is also available in the "Resources" tab online (https://www.apa.org/pubs/books/deliberate-practice-career-counseling). **Do not skip this process!**

How to Assess Difficulty

The career counselor completes the Deliberate Practice Reaction Form (Figure A.1). If they

- rate the difficulty of the exercise above an 8 or had any of the reactions in the "Too Hard" column, follow the instructions to make the exercise easier;

- rate the difficulty of the exercise below a 4 or didn't have any of the reactions in the "Good Challenge" column, proceed to the next level of harder client statements or follow the instructions to make exercise harder; or

- rate the difficulty of the exercise between 4 and 8 and have at least one reaction in the "Good Challenge" column, do not proceed to the harder client statements but rather repeat the same level.

Making Client Statements Easier

If the career counselor ever rates the difficulty of the exercise above an 8 or has any of the reactions in the "Too Hard" column, use the next level easier client statements (e.g., if you were using advanced client statements, switch to intermediate). But if you already were using beginner client statements, use the following methods to make the client statements even easier:

- The person playing the client can use the same beginner client statements but this time in a softer, calmer voice and with a smile. This softens the emotional tone.

FIGURE A.1. Deliberate Practice Reaction Form

Question 1: How challenging was it to fulfill the skill criteria for this exercise?

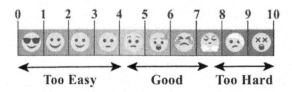

Too Easy — Good — Too Hard

Question 2: Did you have any reactions in "good challenge" or "too hard" categories? (yes/no)					
Good Challenge			**Too Hard**		
Emotions and Thoughts	Body Reactions	Urges	Emotions and Thoughts	Body Reactions	Urges
Manageable shame, self-judgment, irritation, anger, sadness, etc.	Body tension, sighs, shallow breathing, increased heart rate, warmth, dry mouth	Looking away, withdrawing, changing focus	Severe or overwhelming shame, self-judgment, rage, grief, guilt, etc.	Migraines, dizziness, foggy thinking, diarrhea, disassociation, numbness, blanking out, nausea, etc.	Shutting down, giving up

Too Easy	Good Challenge	Too Hard
⬇	⬇	⬇
Proceed to next difficulty level	Repeat the same difficulty level	Go back to previous difficulty level

Note. From *Deliberate Practice in Emotion-Focused Therapy* (p. 180), by R. N. Goldman, A. Vaz, and T. Rousmaniere, 2021, American Psychological Association (https://doi.org/10.1037/0000227-000). Copyright 2021 by the American Psychological Association.

- The client can improvise with topics that are less evocative or make the career counselor more comfortable, such as talking about topics without expressing feelings, the future/past (avoiding the here and now), or any topic outside career counseling (see Figure A.2).

- The career counselor can take a short break (5–10 minutes) between questions.

- The trainer can expand the "feedback phase" by discussing career counseling theory and research. This should shift the trainees' focus toward more detached or intellectual topics and reduce the emotional intensity.

Making Client Statements Harder

If the career counselor rates the difficulty of the exercise below a 4 or didn't have any of the reactions in the "Good Challenge" column, proceed to next-level-harder client statements. If you were already using the advanced client statements, the person playing the client should make the exercise even harder, using the following guidelines:

- The person playing the client can use the advanced client statements again with a more distressed voice (e.g., very angry, sad, sarcastic) or unpleasant facial expression. This should increase the emotional tone.

FIGURE A.2. How to Make Client Statements Easier or Harder in Role-Plays

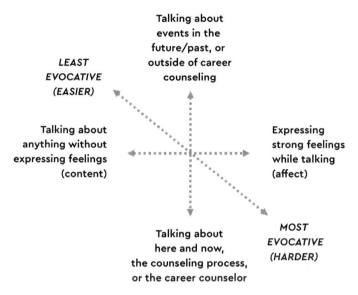

Note. Adapted from figure created by Jason Whipple, PhD.

- The client can improvise new client statements with topics that are more evocative or make the career counselor uncomfortable, such as expressing strong feelings or talking about the here and now, career counseling, or the career counselor (see Figure A.2).

> Note. The purpose of a deliberate practice session is not to get through all the client statements and career counselor responses but rather to spend as much time as possible practicing at the correct difficulty level. This may mean that trainees repeat the same statements and responses many times, which is okay as long as the difficulty remains in the "good challenge" level.

Deliberate Practice Diary Form

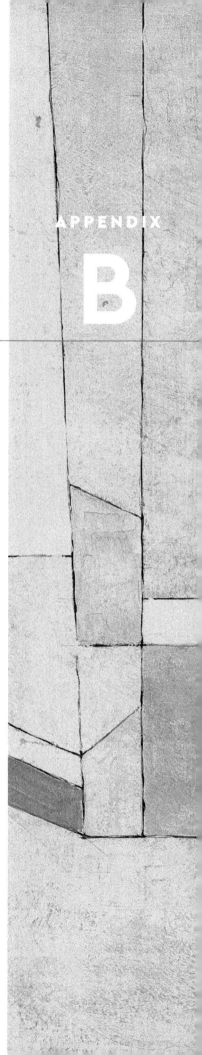

APPENDIX B

This book focuses on deliberate practice methods that involve active, live engagement between trainees and a supervisor. Importantly, deliberate practice can extend beyond these focused training sessions. For example, a trainee might read the client stimuli quietly or aloud and practice their responses independently between sessions with a supervisor. In such cases, it is important for the trainee to speak aloud rather than rehearse silently in one's head. Alternatively, two trainees can practice without the supervisor. Although the absence of a supervisor limits one source of feedback, the peer trainee who is playing the client can serve this role, as they can when a supervisor is present. Importantly, these additional deliberate practice opportunities are intended to take place between focused training sessions with a supervisor. To optimize the quality of the deliberate practice when conducted independently or without a supervisor, we have developed a Deliberate Practice Diary Form that can also be downloaded from the "Resources" tab online (https://www.apa.org/pubs/books/deliberate-practice-career-counseling). This form provides a template for the trainee to record their experience of the deliberate practice activity and, ideally, will aid in the consolidation of learning. This form can also be used as part of the evaluation process with the supervisor but is not necessarily intended for that purpose, and trainees are certainly welcome to bring their experience with the independent practice into the next meeting with the supervisor.

Deliberate Practice Diary Form

Use this form to consolidate learnings from the deliberate practice exercises. Please protect your personal boundaries by only sharing information that you are comfortable disclosing.

Name: _____ Date: _____
Exercise: _____

Question 1. What was helpful or worked well this deliberate practice session? In what way?

Question 2. What was unhelpful or didn't go well this deliberate practice session? In what way?

Question 3. What did you learn about yourself, your current skills, and skills you'd like to keep improving? Feel free to share any details, but only those you are comfortable disclosing.

Sample Career Counseling Syllabus With Embedded Deliberate Practice Exercises

APPENDIX C

This appendix provides a sample one-semester, three-unit course dedicated to teaching career counseling. This course is appropriate for graduate students (master's and doctoral) at all levels of training, including first-year students who have not yet worked with clients. We present it as a model that can be adapted to a specific program's contexts and needs. For example, instructors may borrow portions of it to use in other courses, in practica, in didactic training events at externships and internships, in workshops, and in continuing education for postgraduate therapists and counselors.

Course Title: Career Counseling and Assessment: Theory and Deliberate Practice

Course Description

Welcome to Career Counseling and Assessment: Theory and Deliberate Practice! I am delighted that you are taking this course. This course teaches theory, assessment, and core skills of career counseling. As a course with both didactic and practicum elements, it will review the theory and research on career counseling and assessment and foster the use of deliberate practice to enable students to acquire 10 key career counseling skills. There will be several class activities aimed at meeting the overall goal. Your personal involvement and intellectual investment in the course are the keys to a rewarding class experience. In this course, you will learn about the history of vocational psychology, important vocational theories, assessments, and interventions, landmark research, and current directions in vocational psychology. I will bring you "real-world" examples from my work at the University of Florida's Career Resource Center; the University of Florida, the Ohio State University, Santa Fe College, and West Virginia University's Counseling Centers; a multicultural student center; a psychiatric hospital; a nonprofit counseling center for low-income women and children; and an underserved high school. I'd also like you to consider you own experiences and your experiences with clients who have made or are in the process of making career decisions or clients who are unsatisfied or unsuccessful in their careers. We will look at career counseling through a number of lenses in this course, including multicultural theories, developmental theories, learning theories, and newer theories, such as chaos theory and planned happenstance. We will also talk about logotherapy, discovering your meaning in life, and how to help your clients discover their purposes as

183

well. My goal is to make this course both professionally and personally relevant for you and to encourage you to engage in critical thinking and reflection. Detailed course objectives and relevant competencies are included near the end of the syllabus. Although I hold the role of the professor, I want to emphasize that this is a collective learning experience, and you, as the student, are my most valuable resource for ensuring the course's success and continuous improvement. I genuinely appreciate and eagerly anticipate your feedback and suggestions, and I encourage you to share them openly.

Course Objectives

Students who complete this course will be able to do the following:

1. Describe the core theories, research, and skills related to career counseling.

2. Apply the principles of deliberate practice for career-long career counseling skill development.

3. Demonstrate key career counseling skills.

4. Provide personalized career assessment feedback to clients and integrate themes from career assessment reports into career counseling sessions to spark new insights.

5. Employ career counseling with clients from diverse cultural backgrounds.

6. Support clients experiencing a range of career challenges and assist them in exploring their skills, values, interests, decision-making styles, and cultural and familial influences that impact their career experiences and decisions.

Class Format

Classes are 3 hours long. Course time is split evenly between learning career counseling theory and acquiring career counseling and assessment skills:

Lecture/Discussion Class: Each week, there will be one lecture/discussion class for 1.5 hours focusing on career counseling theory and related research.

Career Counseling Skills Lab: Each week there will be one Career Counseling Skills Lab for 1.5 hours. Skills Labs are for practicing career counseling skills using the exercises in this book. The exercises use career counseling simulations (role-plays) with the following goals:

1. Build trainees' skill and confidence for using career counseling skills with real clients.

2. Provide a safe space for experimenting with different career counseling interventions, without fear of making mistakes.

3. Provide plenty of opportunities to explore and "try on" different skills related to career counseling so that trainees develop a range of career counseling tools to support a diverse client caseload.

Mock Sessions: Twice in the semester (Weeks 12 and 15), trainees will do a career counseling mock session in the Career Counseling Skills Lab. In contrast to highly structured and repetitive deliberate practice exercises, a career counseling mock session is an unstructured and improvised role-played career counseling session. Mock sessions allow trainees to

1. practice using career counseling skills responsively,
2. experiment with career counseling decision making in an unscripted context,
3. discover their personal career counseling style, and
4. build endurance for working with real clients.

Appendix C

Date	Lecture and Discussion	Skills Lab	Homework (due the day of the class)
Week 1	Introduction: history of career counseling and vocational psychology Your professor shares their career lifeline	—	Swanson & Fouad (2019, Chapters 1 & 2); Baker (2009); Savickas & Baker (2005)
Week 2	Critical review of theory of work adjustment and person–environment fit theory	Exercise 1: Exploring your client's skills	Swanson & Fouad (2019, Chapters 7 & 8)
Week 3	Critical review of logotherapy: meaning making in career counseling	Group 1 presents career lifelines Exercise 2: Exploring your client's values	Dik et al. (2015); Lewis et al. (2018); Schultze & Miller (2004); complete career assessments to trade with a partner in 2 weeks
Week 4	Critical review of social cognitive career theory Check-in on the workshop *Bring assessment results to class to trade with a classmate*	Group 2 presents career lifelines Exercise 3: Exploring your client's decision-making styles	Swanson & Fouad (2019, Chapter 11); Brown & Lent (2019)
Week 5	Critical review of the psychology of working theory Current events: careers and the COVID-19 pandemic	Exercise 4: Exploring your client's cultural and familial influences	Swanson & Fouad (2019, Chapter 13); Blustein et al. (2019)
Week 6	Let's prepare for our outreach workshop! Check-in on upcoming midterm exam	Exercise 5: Discussing the benefits of career counseling	No readings this week
Week 7	Critical review of the role of assessment in career development	Exercise 6: Setting session goals Midterm exam	Swanson & Fouad (2019, Chapter 6); Ward & Bingham (1993); Lake et al. (2019)
Week 8	Critical review of lifespan, life-space theory, and other developmental theories How to provide assessment feedback to clients *Bring completed assessment paper to class for mock feedback session*	Exercise 7: Feedback on career assessments	Submit assessment paper through our course website; Swanson & Fouad (2019, Chapter 9)
Week 9	Critical review of career construction Refine workshop and practice for workshop	Group 3 presents their career lifelines Exercise 8: Exploring underlying themes in assessments	Swanson & Fouad (2019, Chapter 12); Barclay (2019); Sampaio et al. (2021)
Week 10	Critical review of planned happenstance and chaos theories	Group 4 presents their career lifelines Exercise 9: Addressing client ambivalence and skepticism	Bright & Pryor (2008); Krumboltz (2009); Schlesinger & Pasquarella Daley (2016)
Week 11	Special topics and populations: children's career development Critical review of circumscription and compromise Gender considerations and career development	Group 5 presents their career lifelines Exercise 10: Assigning homework in career counseling	Swanson & Fouad (2019, Chapters 3 & 10); Bell (2018); Betz (2023); Lindo et al. (2022); Santos et al. (2021)
Week 12	Special topics and populations: LGBTQIA+ and BIPOC clients Prepare for social justice workshop	Group 6 presents their career lifelines Mock counseling session Prepare for social justice workshop	Swanson & Fouad (2019, Chapters 4 & 5); Byars Winston & Fouad (2006); Cadenas et al. (2020); Chung et al. (2015); Singh & Moss (2016)
Week 13	Provide social justice workshop in the community *Around this week or so, we will present a workshop in the community to support those who are experiencing unemployment.*	Community workshop	No readings this week
Week 14	Process social justice workshop experience Professional development: preparing for your job market Course wrap-up	Choose Your Own Adventure Day! Repeat the exercise you've found most challenging thus far in the semester, so you can engage in some additional practice.	Optional professional development readings posted on our course website
Week 15	Final exam Self-evaluation and skill coaching feedback Course evaluations	Mock session and self-evaluation	No reading this week

Homework

During the semester, you will present (a) your career lifeline, (b) vocational assessment results to your partner, and (c) a social justice/community workshop. To prepare you for the licensure exam, you will also complete a midterm and final exam. More information about each of these course requirements follows.

Career Journey Presentation

This presentation will offer you a unique opportunity to share your personal career development journey with the others in our class. You will explore the various career paths you've considered or taken and the evolution that has led you to your current point. Reflect on your career aspirations, past experiences, and your present plans. Identify the individuals, locations, cultures, and events that have played a pivotal role in shaping your experiences and decisions. While doing so, be on the lookout for recurring themes, significant turning points, and your future ambitions and goals. The primary objective of this presentation is to share with others a wide-spanning account of the multifaceted factors that have contributed to your current position in your career and your envisioned future career path. Please prepare a brief presentation of your career journey to share with four or five classmates and me. Presentations should last approximately 20 minutes, with an additional 5 to 10 minutes for questions and answers. You will also submit a brief, one-page paper addressing the topics mentioned previously. As the semester progresses, think about how your career story ties in with different vocational theories and which one(s) you resonate with most. Please sign up for your presentation by Week 2 of class. You can sign up on the course website. I will share my career journey with you on our first week of class.

Vocational Assessment Paper

To familiarize yourself with some common career assessments, you will participate in two self-assessments: a career interest inventory and a personality inventory. It is recommended that you answer the questions candidly for the most beneficial experience. However, if you are uncomfortable doing so, you have the option to approach the assessment from the perspective of a "client" (channel your inner friend, family member, or past client and take the assessments as you believe they would have). You can complete this activity at your convenience, whether it be in the library, at home, or any other suitable location. Two self-assessment tests we recommend you take are the Strong Interest Inventory (SII) and the Myers–Briggs Type Indicator (MBTI). However, many other tests can be used for this assignment, so feel free to ask for or propose alternatives to your teacher. While taking the actual assessments is recommended (we will discuss this further in class), I understand the financial constraints often faced in graduate school. A similar free career interest inventory and a free online personality assessment similar to the MBTI can be accessed on the course website. Please complete the inventories by the start of class on Week 4 (but don't wait until the last minute! Computers/the internet seems to sense when we are under pressure and tends to choose that moment to malfunction!). Bring your assessment results to class on Week 4 to exchange with a classmate. You will analyze and interpret the results of your partner's inventories and create a short written report on the results. The report should be approximately two pages, single-spaced, and should include the following items:

- **Clear Explanation of Career Inventory Codes (30 points):** Provide a straightforward explanation of the assessment codes, avoiding psychology jargon as much as possible. For example, instead of saying the client is "introverted," clarify what "introverted" means.

- **Data Analysis and Creative Thinking (25 points):** Analyze the assessment data and discuss their implications for the careers and work environments that may be best suited for your "client." This is an opportunity to explore creative ideas and demonstrate how the results of the interest assessment and personality assessment complement each other.

- **Strength of Personality Preferences (3 points):** Explain the strength of your "client's" personality preferences.

- **Strength of Interest Areas (3 points):** Describe the strength of your "client's" interest areas.

- **Noting Limited Career Representation (2 points):** Acknowledge that the careers listed in the inventories are only a subset of a range of potential suitable options.

- **Explanation of Assessment Scope (2 points):** Explain what the inventories measure and what they do not measure, distinguishing between, for example, interests and skills.

- **Personalized Recommendations Grounded in Theory (25 points):** On the basis of the information from the interest and personality inventories, provide personalized recommendations as if you were counseling a client. Ensure that your recommendations are supported by relevant theoretical frameworks.

- **Professionalism and Accuracy (10 points):** Maintain a professional standard in your paper, free from grammar and spelling errors.

You can find sample reports on our course website for reference. This paper will be due on Week 8. On that day, you will partner with your "client" and will offer feedback on the results.

Social Justice Workshop

You will work with two or three other students in class and will develop and present a workshop to members of our community who are currently unemployed and looking to enter or reenter the workplace. We will determine in small groups where we would like to focus our efforts. Your responsibility is to take an active role in this approximately 30- to 60-minute workshop. We will cover a topic of our choosing, based on the needs of the organization and in conjunction with consultations with their staff; some examples might include stress management, work–life balance, or forgiveness at work, or we could focus on a skill-building workshop, such as interview skills, resume writing, and so on. This workshop will require planning outside of class, but we will set aside a limited amount of class time to get started and to practice. This social justice workshop will most likely take place on Week 13. Because I anticipate it will be difficult to coordinate all of our schedules, we will try to hold the workshop during class toward the end of the semester. Additionally, because we have a large class, we will likely work on five to six social justice workshops. The number of workshops we provide will largely depend on the populations you're interested in working with and the format of their organization. These time frames and the number of workshops may need to be flexible until we start our planning on Week 4. We will discuss this in more detail in class, and you will be able to add this professional service activity to your vitae.

Midterm and Final Exams

These exams are designed to prepare you for your licensure exam (master's students) and your qualifying exam (doctoral students) and are intended for you to demonstrate your mastery of the content (e.g., your understanding of the major career theories, how they are integrated in career counseling, what interventions are commonly used). The tests will consist of a combination of multiple choice and short answer items.

Multicultural Orientation

This course is taught in a multicultural context, defined as "how the cultural worldviews, values, and beliefs of the client and therapist interact and influence one another to co-create a relational experience that is in the spirit of healing" (Davis et al., 2018, p. 3). Throughout this course, students are encouraged to apply a multicultural orientation framework by engaging in cultural humility; responding to discussions about culture in an open, calm, and nondefensive manner; and attuning to cultural opportunities (Hook et al., 2017). While several class sessions will concentrate on addressing unique career considerations related to specific demographic groups (e.g., LGBTQIA+ clients, women, men, children, clients from diverse ethnic and racial backgrounds), I aim to weave multicultural considerations into each class discussion. This is especially critical because both you and your clients will encompass diverse intersecting identities that merit thoughtful consideration. For further guidance on this topic and deliberate practice exercises to improve multicultural skills, see the book *Deliberate Practice in Multicultural Therapy* (Harris et al., 2024).

Vulnerability, Privacy, and Boundaries

This course is aimed at developing career counseling skills, self-awareness, and interpersonal skills in an experiential framework and as relevant to clinical work. This course is not psychotherapy or a substitute for psychotherapy. Students should interact at a level of self-disclosure that is personally comfortable and helpful to their own learning. Although becoming aware of internal emotional and psychological processes is necessary for a career counselor's development, it is not necessary to reveal all that information to the trainer. It is important for students to sense their own level of safety and privacy. Students are not evaluated on the level of material that they choose to reveal in the class.

In accordance with the *Ethical Principles of Psychologists and Code of Conduct* (American Psychological Association [APA], 2017), **students are not required to disclose personal information.** Because this class is about developing both interpersonal and career counseling competence, following are some important points so that students are fully informed as they make choices to self-disclose:

- Students choose how much, when, and what to disclose. Students are not penalized for choosing not to share personal information.

- The learning environment is susceptible to group dynamics much like any other group space, and therefore students may be asked to share their observations and experiences of the class environment with the singular goal of fostering a more inclusive and productive learning environment.

Confidentiality

To create a safe learning environment that is respectful of client and counselor information and diversity and to foster open and vulnerable conversation in class, students are required to agree to strict confidentiality within and outside of the instruction setting.

Evaluation

Self-Evaluation: At the end of the semester (Week 15), trainees will perform a self-evaluation. This will help trainees track their progress and identify areas for further development. The Guidance for Trainees section in Chapter 3 of this book highlights potential areas of focus for self-evaluation.

Grades

Course grades are assigned based on the percentage of points earned (i.e., mastery of the course material), rather than on a curve. Final grades are based on a total of 550 points. **Note that I do not curve.** If you get 516 points, that is an A–, not an A. Your grades will be posted on our course website.

The breakdown of point percentages and grades associated with total points earned is as follows:

Career Lifeline	50 points
Career Assessment Paper	100 points
Midterm Exam	100 points
Social Justice Community Workshop	100 points
Final Exam	100 points
Participation and Professionalism	100 points

Percentage/Points	Grades
94%–100% (517–550 pts)	A
90%–93% (495–516 pts)	A–
87%–89% (478–494 pts)	B+
84%–86% (462–477 pts)	B
80%–83% (440–461 pts)	B–
77%–79% (424–439 pts)	C+
74%–76% (407–423 pts)	C
70%–73% (385–406 pts)	C–
69% or below (384 pts or less)	F

Course Objectives and Competency Goals

In alignment with the Cube Model of Professional Development (Rodolfa et al., 2005), students will gain knowledge of and competence in the following areas.

Foundational Competencies: Students will demonstrate understanding of traditional and emerging theories and methods of career counseling. These domains of competence are as follows:

- *Reflective Practice/Self-Assessment/Self-Care:* You will demonstrate personal development as aspiring counseling psychologists in self-awareness, a commitment to social justice, and compassion. You will engage in self-reflection regarding your attitudes, values, and beliefs toward diverse clients and will explore your impact on others through class discussions and assignments. You will self-identify multiple individual and cultural identities through class discussions, your career lifeline, your assessment report, and your self-evaluation in Week 15. You will also be encouraged to engage in self-care as an important component of professionalism. You will be encouraged to engage in self-reflection and personal growth by exploring your career path and experiences that have led you to a career in the field of counseling psychology. You will also demonstrate an understanding of the complex challenges that accompany exploration of careers, particularly in relation to an individual's life experiences, societal impacts, values, skills, personality, familial impacts, self-efficacy beliefs and outcome expectations, and purpose in life.

- **Scientific Knowledge and Methods:** You will gain knowledge of relevant research on career counseling and career theories and will be encouraged to engage in critical thinking regarding empirically sound interventions in career counseling and empirically driven theories. You will explore the strengths and weaknesses of each theory, and you will also demonstrate a working knowledge and understanding of career development concepts through in-class assignments, presentations, and assigned papers.

- **Interpersonal Relationship Skills:** You will gain knowledge of career counseling techniques to increase the working alliance between yourself and your career clients, particularly through our Career Counseling Skills Lab.

- **Ethical and Legal Standards:** You will learn about the APA's (2017) ethical and legal standards, in addition to ethical standards set by the National Career Development Association and the American Counseling Association.

- **Individual and Cultural Diversity:** You will gain multicultural knowledge to work effectively with clients from diverse backgrounds, including working with LGBTQIA+ clients, men and women, clients with disabilities, low-income clients, and clients from diverse ethnic and racial backgrounds. You will explore the ways in which social barriers interact with working and impact clinical concerns. You will consider the relevancy of career counseling theories and research in relation to certain groups. You will also explore your own privilege, assumptions, and biases in class, as relevant and important for working with diverse clients.

- **Interdisciplinary Systems:** In this course, you will gain knowledge about working with professionals in career counseling contexts who are trained in the areas of social work, counseling, and marketing.

Functional Competencies: Students will demonstrate the ability to work effectively as beginning counseling psychologists with diverse populations.

- **Assessment Skills:** You will learn how to apply several vocational assessments (e.g., MBTI, SII, Values Card Sort, Focus-2) to various career concerns. You will also learn how to integrate personality and interest assessments effectively into a meaningful, comprehensive picture of your clients and their career concerns. I will demonstrate my techniques for providing career counseling assessment feedback, and you will also have the opportunity to provide feedback to a classmate (and receive feedback from me).

- **Research and Evaluation Skills:** You will learn about critical research in career counseling and research that relates to specific theories of career counseling. Through the class discussions, you will be asked to evaluate the effectiveness of the relevant research of the assigned readings.

- ***Intervention Skills:*** You will be provided with opportunities in each class to enhance your ability to think effectively and creatively about your clients' work-related problems. You will develop a working knowledge and skills to use various career-related interventions because most applicable for clients from diverse backgrounds and clients with diverse presenting concerns. You will also have multiple in-class opportunities to both observe and participate in interventions based on theories discussed in class and interventions taught through our Skills Lab.

- ***Supervision/Teaching Skills:*** You will advance your teaching skills and knowledge about theories and assessments through class discussions and demonstrating application of theories to your classmates. You will also learn about several useful resources (e.g., websites, free assessment tools, books and articles) to share with your clients and to use in career counseling sessions to enhance career exploration.

Continuing Competencies: Students will be encouraged to engage in, and develop, a lifelong curiosity for learning and the important role of work in human development.

Attendance Policy

This course will be interactive, and each week we will be covering a new theory or theories. Students are expected to attend class, be on time, and actively participate. When you are absent, you miss out on opportunities to integrate theories into practice. Recognizing that life happens and things can come up, two excused absences are permitted. As much as you are able, out of professional courtesy, please contact me before class to let me know you will be absent.

Consistent with our university's guidelines, students absent from regularly scheduled examinations because of authorized university activities will have the opportunity to take them at an alternate time. Make-up exams for absences due to any other reason will be at the discretion of the instructor.

Required Textbook

Swanson, L. L., & Fouad, N. A. (2019). *Career theory and practice: Learning through case studies* (4th ed.). Sage Publications.

Required Articles and Book Chapters

Baker, D. B. (2009). Choosing a vocation at 100: Time, change, and context. *The Career Development Quarterly, 57*(3), 199–206. https://doi.org/10.1002/j.2161-0045.2009.tb00105.x

Barclay, S. R. (2019). Creative use of the career construction interview. *The Career Development Quarterly, 67*(2), 126–138. https://doi.org/10.1002/cdq.12176

Bell, T. J. (2018). Career counseling with Black men: Applying principles of existential psychotherapy. *The Career Development Quarterly, 66*(2), 162–175. https://doi.org/10.1002/cdq.12130

Betz, N. E. (2023). Integrating 50 years of theory and research: Suggestions for directions on women's career development. *The Counseling Psychologist, 51*(6), 849–861. https://doi.org/10.1177/00110000231176246

Blustein, D. L., Kenny, M. E., Autin, K., & Duffy, R. (2019). The psychology of working in practice: A theory of change for a new era. *The Career Development Quarterly, 67*(3), 236–264. https://doi.org/10.1002/cdq.12193

Bright, J. E. H., & Pryor, R. G. L. (2008). Shiftwork: A chaos theory of careers agenda for change in career counseling. *Australian Journal of Career Development, 17*(3), 63–72. https://doi.org/10.1177/103841620801700309

Brown, S. D., & Lent, R. W. (2019). Social cognitive career theory at 25: Progress in studying the domain satisfaction and career self-management models. *Journal of Career Assessment, 27*(4), 563–578. https://doi.org/10.1177/1069072719852736

Byars-Winston, A. M., & Fouad, N. A. (2006). Metacognition and multicultural competence: Expanding the culturally appropriate career counseling model. *The Career Development Quarterly, 54*(3), 187–201. https://doi.org/10.1002/j.2161-0045.2006.tb00151.x

Cadenas, G. A., Lynn, N., Li, K. M., Liu, L., Cantú, E. A., Ruth, A., Carroll, S., Kulp, S., & Spence, T. (2020). Racial/ethnic minority community college students' critical consciousness and social cognitive career outcomes. *The Career Development Quarterly, 68*(4), 302–317. https://doi.org/10.1002/cdq.12238

Chung, Y. B., Chang, T. K., & Rose, C. S. (2015, February 16). *Managing and coping with sexual identity at work.* The British Psychological Society. https://www.bps.org.uk/psychologist/managing-and-coping-sexual-identity-work

Dik, B. J., Duffy, R. D., Allan, B. A., O'Donnell, M. B., Shim, Y., & Steger, M. F. (2015). Purpose and meaning in career development applications. *The Counseling Psychologist, 43*(4), 558–585. https://doi.org/10.1177/0011000014546872

Krumboltz, J. D. (2009). The happenstance learning theory. *Journal of Career Assessment, 17*(2), 135–154. https://doi.org/10.1177/1069072708328861

Lake, C. J., Carlson, J., Rose, A., & Chlevin-Thiele, C. (2019). Trust in name brand assessments: The case of the Myers–Briggs Type Indicator. *The Psychologist-Manager Journal, 22*(2), 91–107. https://doi.org/10.1037/mgr0000086

Lewis, J. A., Raque-Bogdan, T. L., Lee, S., & Rao, M. (2018). Examining the role of ethnic identity and meaning in life on career decision-making self-efficacy. *Journal of Career Development, 45*(1), 68–82. https://doi.org/10.1177/0894845317696803

Lindo, N. A., Li, D., Hastings, T., Ceballos, P., Werts, R., Molina, C., Oller, M., & Laird, A. (2022). Child and adolescent career construction: Lived experiences of an expressive arts group. *The Career Development Quarterly, 70*(4), 300–313. https://doi.org/10.1002/cdq.12307

Sampaio, C., Cardoso, P., Rossier, J., & Savickas, M. L. (2021). Attending to clients' psychological needs during career construction counseling. *The Career Development Quarterly, 69*(2), 96–113. https://doi.org/10.1002/cdq.12252

Santos, T. C., Mann, E. S., & Pfeffer, C. A. (2021). Are university health services meeting the needs of transgender college students? A qualitative assessment of a public university. *Journal of American College Health, 69*(1), 59–66. https://doi.org/10.1080/07448481.2019.1652181

Savickas, M. L., & Baker, D. B. (2005). The history of vocational psychology: Antecedents, origin, and early development. In W. B. Walsh & M. L. Savickas (Eds.), *Handbook of vocational psychology: Theory, research, and practice* (pp. 15–50). Lawrence Erlbaum Associates.

Schlesinger, J., & Pasquarella Daley, L. (2016). Applying the chaos theory of careers as a framework for college career centers. *Journal of Employment Psychology, 53*(2), 86–96. https://doi.org/10.1002/joec.12030

Schultze, G., & Miller, C. M. (2004). The search for meaning and career development. *Career Development International, 9*(2), 142–152. https://doi.org/10.1108/13620430410526184

Singh, A. A., & Moss, L. (2016). Using relational-cultural theory in LGBTQQ counseling: Addressing heterosexism and enhancing relational competencies. *Journal of Counseling & Development, 94*(4), 398–404. https://doi.org/10.1002/jcad.12098

Ward, C. M., & Bingham, R. P. (1993). Career assessment of ethnic minority women. *Journal of Career Assessment, 1*(3), 246–257. https://doi.org/10.1177/106907279300100304

References

Abramson, A. (2022). Burnout and stress are everywhere. *Monitor on Psychology*, 53(1), 72.

American Psychological Association. (2017). *Ethical principles of psychologists and code of conduct* (2002, Amended June 1, 2010, and January 1, 2017). https://www.apa.org/ethics/code/

American Psychological Association. (2021). *The American workforce faces compounding pressure: APA's 2021 Work and Well-Being Survey results*. https://www.apa.org/pubs/reports/work-well-being/compounding-pressure-2021

Anderson, T., Ogles, B. M., Patterson, C. L., Lambert, M. J., & Vermeersch, D. A. (2009). Therapist effects: Facilitative interpersonal skills as a predictor of therapist success. *Journal of Clinical Psychology*, 65(7), 755–768. https://doi.org/10.1002/jclp.20583

Andreassen, C. S. (2014). Workaholism: An overview and current status of the research. *Journal of Behavioral Addictions*, 3(1), 1–11. https://doi.org/10.1556/JBA.2.2013.017

Bailey, R. J., & Ogles, B. M. (2019). Common factors as a therapeutic approach: What is required? *Practice Innovations*, 4(4), 241–254. https://doi.org/10.1037/pri0000100

Baker, D. B. (2009). Choosing a vocation at 100: Time, change, and context. *The Career Development Quarterly*, 57(3), 199–206. https://doi.org/10.1002/j.2161-0045.2009.tb00105.x

Barclay, S. R. (2019). Creative use of the career construction interview. *The Career Development Quarterly*, 67(2), 126–138. https://doi.org/10.1002/cdq.12176

Barlow, D. H. (2010). Negative effects from psychological treatments: A perspective. *American Psychologist*, 65(1), 13–20. https://doi.org/10.1037/a0015643

Bell, T. J. (2018). Career counseling with Black men: Applying principles of existential psychotherapy. *The Career Development Quarterly*, 66(2), 162–175. https://doi.org/10.1002/cdq.12130

Bennett-Levy, J. (2019). Why therapists should walk the talk: The theoretical and empirical case for personal practice in therapist training and professional development. *Journal of Behavior Therapy and Experimental Psychiatry*, 62, 133–145. https://doi.org/10.1016/j.jbtep.2018.08.004

Bennett-Levy, J., & Finlay-Jones, A. (2018). The role of personal practice in therapist skill development: A model to guide therapists, educators, supervisors and researchers. *Cognitive Behaviour Therapy*, 47(3), 185–205. https://doi.org/10.1080/16506073.2018.1434678

Betz, N. E. (2023). Integrating 50 years of theory and research: Suggestions for directions on women's career development. *The Counseling Psychologist*, 51(6), 849–861. https://doi.org/10.1177/00110000231176246

Blustein, D. L., Kenny, M. E., Autin, K., & Duffy, R. (2019). The psychology of working in practice: A theory of change for a new era. *The Career Development Quarterly*, 67(3), 236–254. https://doi.org/10.1002/cdq.12193

Bohart, A. C., & Wade, A. G. (2013). The client in psychotherapy. In M. J. Lambert (Ed.), *Bergin and Garfield's handbook of psychotherapy and behavior change* (5th ed., pp. 13–43). John Wiley & Sons.

Bravata, D. M., Watts, S. A., Keefer, A. L., Madhusudhan, D. K., Taylor, K. T., Clark, D. M., Nelson, R. S., Cokley, K. O., & Hagg, H. K. (2020). Prevalence, predictors, and treatment of imposter syndrome: A systematic review. *Journal of General Internal Medicine, 35*(4), 1252–1275. https://doi.org/10.1007/s11606-019-05364-1

Bright, J. E. H., & Pryor, R. G. L. (2008). Shiftwork: A chaos theory of careers agenda for change in career counseling. *Australian Journal of Career Development, 17*(3), 63–72. https://doi.org/10.1177/103841620801700309

Brown, S. D., & Lent, R. W. (2019). Social cognitive career theory at 25: Progress in studying the domain satisfaction and career self-management models. *Journal of Career Assessment, 27*(4), 563–578. https://doi.org/10.1177/1069072719852736

Bugatti, M., & Boswell, J. F. (2016). Clinical errors as a lack of context responsiveness. *Psychotherapy: Theory, Research, & Practice, 53*(3), 262–267. https://doi.org/10.1037/pst0000080

Bullock-Yowell, E., McConnell, A. E., & Schedin, E. A. (2014). Decided and undecided students: Career self-efficacy, negative thinking, and decision-making difficulties. *NACADA Journal, 34*(1), 22–34. https://doi.org/10.12930/NACADA-13-016

Byars-Winston, A. M., & Fouad, N. A. (2006). Metacognition and multicultural competence: Expanding the culturally appropriate career counseling model. *The Career Development Quarterly, 54*(3), 187–201. https://doi.org/10.1002/j.2161-0045.2006.tb00151.x

Cadenas, G. A., Lynn, N., Li, K. M., Liu, L., Cantú, E. A., Ruth, A., Carroll, S., Kulp, S., & Spence, T. (2020). Racial/ethnic minority community college students' critical consciousness and social cognitive career outcomes. *The Career Development Quarterly, 68*(4), 302–317. https://doi.org/10.1002/cdq.12238

Castonguay, L. G., Goldfried, M. R., Wiser, S., Raue, P. J., & Hayes, A. M. (1996). Predicting the effect of cognitive therapy for depression: A study of unique and common factors. *Journal of Consulting and Clinical Psychology, 64*(3), 497–504. https://doi.org/10.1037/0022-006X.64.3.497

Chung, Y. B., Chang, T. K., & Rose, C. S. (2015, February 16). *Managing and coping with sexual identity at work*. The British Psychological Society. https://www.bps.org.uk/psychologist/managing-and-coping-sexual-identity-work

Clark, D., & Molinsky, A. (2014, March 21). Self-promotion for professionals from countries where bragging is bad. *Harvard Business Review*. https://hbr.org/2014/03/self-promotion-for-professionals-from-countries-where-bragging-is-bad

Clark, M., Vardeman, K., & Barba, S. (2014). Perceived inadequacy: A study of the imposter phenomenon among college and research librarians. *College & Research Libraries, 75*(3), 255–271. https://doi.org/10.5860/crl12-423

Coker, J. (1990). *How to practice jazz*. Jamey Aebersold.

Cook, R. (2005). *It's about that time: Miles Davis on and off record*. Atlantic Books.

Csikszentmihalyi, M. (1997). *Finding flow: The psychology of engagement with everyday life*. HarperCollins.

Dana Ménard, A., & Chittle, L. (2023). The imposter phenomenon in post-secondary students: A review of the literature. *Review of Education, 11*(2), Article e3399. https://doi.org/10.1002/rev3.3399

Davis, D. E., DeBlaere, C., Owen, J., Hook, J. N., Rivera, D. P., Choe, E., Van Tongeren, D. R., Worthington, E. L., Jr., & Placeres, V. (2018). The multicultural orientation framework: A narrative review. *Psychotherapy, 55*(1), 89–100. https://doi.org/10.1037/pst0000160

Dik, B. J., Duffy, R. D., Allan, B. A., O'Donnell, M. B., Shim, Y., & Steger, M. F. (2015). Purpose and meaning in career development applications. *The Counseling Psychologist, 43*(4), 558–585. https://doi.org/10.1177/0011000014546872

Duffy, R. D., & Sedlacek, W. E. (2007). The presence of and search for a calling: Connections to career development. *Journal of Vocational Behavior, 70*(3), 590–601. https://doi.org/10.1016/j.jvb.2007.03.007

Edwards, J. (2018). Counseling and psychology student experiences of personal therapy: A critical interpretive synthesis. *Frontiers in Psychology, 9*, Article 1732. https://doi.org/10.3389/fpsyg.2018.01732

Ellis, M. V., Berger, L., Hanus, A. E., Ayala, E. E., Swords, B. A., & Siembor, M. (2014). Inadequate and harmful clinical supervision: Testing a revised framework and assessing occurrence. *The Counseling Psychologist, 42*(4), 434–472. https://doi.org/10.1177/0011000013508656

Ericsson, K. A. (2003). Development of elite performance and deliberate practice: An update from the perspective of the expert performance approach. In J. L. Starkes & K. A. Ericsson (Eds.), *Expert performance in sports: Advances in research on sport expertise* (pp. 49–83). Human Kinetics.

Ericsson, K. A. (2004). Deliberate practice and the acquisition and maintenance of expert performance in medicine and related domains: Invited address. *Academic Medicine, 79*(Suppl. 10), S70–S81. https://doi.org/10.1097/00001888-200410001-00022

Ericsson, K. A. (2006). The influence of experience and deliberate practice on the development of superior expert performance. In K. A. Ericsson, N. Charness, P. J. Feltovich, & R. R. Hoffman (Eds.), *The Cambridge handbook of expertise and expert performance* (pp. 683–703). Cambridge University Press. https://doi.org/10.1017/CBO9780511816796.038

Ericsson, K. A., Hoffman, R. R., Kozbelt, A., & Williams, A. M. (Eds.). (2018). *The Cambridge handbook of expertise and expert performance* (2nd ed.). Cambridge University Press. https://doi.org/10.1017/9781316480748

Ericsson, K. A., Krampe, R. T., & Tesch-Römer, C. (1993). The role of deliberate practice in the acquisition of expert performance. *Psychological Review, 100*(3), 363–406. https://doi.org/10.1037/0033-295X.100.3.363

Ericsson, K. A., & Pool, R. (2016). *Peak: Secrets from the new science of expertise*. Houghton Mifflin Harcourt.

Fisher, R. P., & Craik, F. I. M. (1977). Interaction between encoding and retrieval operations in cued recall. *Journal of Experimental Psychology: Human Learning and Memory, 3*(6), 701–711. https://doi.org/10.1037/0278-7393.3.6.701

Flores, L. Y., & Bike, D. H. (2014). Multicultural career counseling. In F. T. L. Leong, L. Comas-Díaz, G. C. Nagayama Hall, V. C. McLoyd, & J. E. Trimble (Eds.), *APA handbook of multicultural psychology: Vol. 2. Applications and training* (pp. 403–417). American Psychological Association. https://doi.org/10.1037/14187-023

Gati, I., & Levin, N. (2014). Counseling for career decision-making difficulties: Measures and methods. *The Career Development Quarterly, 62*(2), 98–113. https://doi.org/10.1002/j.2161-0045.2014.00073.x

Gladwell, M. (2008). *Outliers: The story of success*. Little, Brown & Co.

Goldberg, S. B., Rousmaniere, T., Miller, S. D., Whipple, J., Nielsen, S. L., Hoyt, W. T., & Wampold, B. E. (2016). Do psychotherapists improve with time and experience? A longitudinal analysis of outcomes in a clinical setting. *Journal of Counseling Psychology, 63*(1), 1–11. https://doi.org/10.1037/cou0000131

Goldman, R. N., Vaz, A., & Rousmaniere, T. (2021). *Deliberate practice in emotion-focused therapy*. American Psychological Association. https://doi.org/10.1037/0000227-000

Goodyear, R. K. (2015). Using accountability mechanisms more intentionally: A framework and its implications for training professional psychologists. *American Psychologist, 70*(8), 736–743. https://doi.org/10.1037/a0039828

Goodyear, R. K., & Nelson, M. L. (1997). The major formats of psychotherapy supervision. In C. E. Watkins, Jr. (Ed.), *Handbook of psychotherapy supervision* (pp. 328–334). John Wiley & Sons.

Greenberg, L. S., & Goldman, R. L. (1988). Training in experiential therapy. *Journal of Consulting and Clinical Psychology, 56*(5), 696–702. https://doi.org/10.1037/0022-006X.56.5.696

Haggerty, G., & Hilsenroth, M. J. (2011). The use of video in psychotherapy supervision. *British Journal of Psychotherapy, 27*(2), 193–210. https://doi.org/10.1111/j.1752-0118.2011.01232.x

Harris, J., Jin, J., Hoffman, S., Phan, S., Prout, T. A., Rousmaniere, T., & Vaz, A. (2024). *Deliberate practice in multicultural therapy*. American Psychological Association. https://doi.org/10.1037/0000357-000

Hatcher, R. L. (2015). Interpersonal competencies: Responsiveness, technique, and training in psychotherapy. *American Psychologist, 70*(8), 747–757. https://doi.org/10.1037/a0039803

Henry, W. P., Strupp, H. H., Butler, S. F., Schacht, T. E., & Binder, J. L. (1993). Effects of training in time-limited dynamic psychotherapy: Changes in therapist behavior. *Journal of Consulting and Clinical Psychology*, *61*(3), 434–440. https://doi.org/10.1037/0022-006X.61.3.434

Hill, C. E., Kivlighan, D. M., III, Rousmaniere, T., Kivlighan, D. M., Jr., Gerstenblith, J. A., & Hillman, J. W. (2020). Deliberate practice for the skill of immediacy: A multiple case study of doctoral student therapists and clients. *Psychotherapy*, *57*(4), 587–597. https://doi.org/10.1037/pst0000247

Hill, C. E., & Knox, S. (2013). Training and supervision in psychotherapy: Evidence for effective practice. In M. J. Lambert (Ed.), *Handbook of psychotherapy and behavior change* (6th ed., pp. 775–811). Wiley.

Hook, J. N., Davis, D. D., Owen, J., & DeBlaere, C. (2017). *Cultural humility: Engaging diverse identities in therapy*. American Psychological Association. https://doi.org/10.1037/0000037-000

Jashinsky, T. L., & King, C. L. (2019, February 1). *Fostering career counseling self-efficacy in counselor education*. Career Convergence Web Magazine, National Career Development Association. https://www.ncda.org/aws/NCDA/pt/sd/news_article/212500/_PARENT/CC_layout_details/false

Jones, L. K. (1994). Frank Parsons' contributions to career counseling. *Journal of Career Development*, *20*(4), 287–294. https://doi.org/10.1177/089484539402000403

Kendall, P. C., & Beidas, R. S. (2007). Smoothing the trail for dissemination of evidence-based practices for youth: Flexibility within fidelity. *Professional Psychology: Research and Practice*, *38*(1), 13–20. https://doi.org/10.1037/0735-7028.38.1.13

Kendall, P. C., & Frank, H. E. (2018). Implementing evidence-based treatment protocols: Flexibility within fidelity. *Clinical Psychology*, *25*(4), e12271. https://doi.org/10.1111/cpsp.12271

Koziol, L. F., & Budding, D. E. (2012). Procedural learning. In Seel N. M. (Ed.), *Encyclopedia of the sciences of learning* (pp. 2694-2696). Springer. https://doi.org/10.1007/978-1-4419-1428-6_670

Krumboltz, J. D. (2009). The happenstance learning theory. *Journal of Career Assessment*, *17*(2), 135–154. https://doi.org/10.1177/1069072708328861

Lake, C. J., Carlson, J., Rose, A., & Chlevin-Thiele, C. (2019). Trust in name brand assessments: The case of the Myers-Briggs Type Indicator. *The Psychologist Manager Journal*, *22*(2), 91–107. https://doi.org/10.1037/mgr0000086

Lambert, M. J. (2010). Yes, it is time for clinicians to monitor treatment outcome. In B. L. Duncan, S. C. Miller, B. E. Wampold, & M. A. Hubble (Eds.), *Heart and soul of change: Delivering what works in therapy* (2nd ed., pp. 239–266). American Psychological Association. https://doi.org/10.1037/12075-008

Lewis, J. A., Raque-Bogdan, T. L., Lee, S., & Rao, M. (2018). Examining the role of ethnic identity and meaning in life on career decision-making self-efficacy. *Journal of Career Development*, *45*(1), 68–82. https://doi.org/10.1177/0894845317696803

Lindo, N. A., Li, D., Hastings, T., Ceballos, P., Werts, R., Molina, C., Oller, M., & Laird, A. (2022). Child and adolescent career construction: Lived experiences of an expressive arts group. *The Career Development Quarterly*, *70*(4), 300–313. https://doi.org/10.1002/cdq.12307

Manuel, J. K., Ernst, D., Vaz, A., & Rousmaniere, T. (2022). *Deliberate practice in motivational interviewing*. American Psychological Association. https://doi.org/10.1037/0000297-000

Mariska, M. A., & Harrawood, L. K. (2013). Understanding the unsaid: Enhancing multicultural competence through nonverbal awareness. *VISTAS Online*, *3*(64), 1–12.

Markman, K. D., & Tetlock, P. E. (2000). Accountability and close-call counterfactuals: The loser who nearly won and the winner who nearly lost. *Personality and Social Psychology Bulletin*, *26*(10), 1213–1224. https://doi.org/10.1177/0146167200262004

Maslach, C., & Leiter, M. P. (2016). Understanding the burnout experience: Recent research and its implications for psychiatry. *World Psychiatry*, *15*(2), 103–111. https://doi.org/10.1002/wps.20311

McGaghie, W. C., Issenberg, S. B., Barsuk, J. H., & Wayne, D. B. (2014). A critical review of simulation-based mastery learning with translational outcomes. *Medical Education*, *48*(4), 375–385. https://doi.org/10.1111/medu.12391

McLeod, J. (2017). Qualitative methods for routine outcome measurement. In T. G. Rousmaniere, R. Goodyear, D. D. Miller, & B. E. Wampold (Eds.), *The cycle of excellence: Using deliberate practice to improve supervision and training* (pp. 99–122). John Wiley & Sons. https://doi.org/10.1002/9781119165590.ch5

Metcalfe, J. (2017). Learning from errors. *Annual Review of Psychology, 68*(1), 465–489. https://doi.org/10.1146/annurev-psych-010416-044022

Mitzkovitz, C., Dowd, S. M., Cothran, T., & Musil, S. (2022). The eyes have it: Psychotherapy in the era of masks. *Journal of Clinical Psychology in Medical Settings, 29*(4), 886–897. https://doi.org/10.1007/s10880-022-09856-x

Morgan, L. W., Greenwaldt, M. E., & Gosselin, K. P. (2014). School counselors' perception of competency in career counseling. *The Professional Counselor, 4*(5), 481–496. https://doi.org/10.15241/lwm.4.5.481

Norcross, J. C., & Guy, J. D. (2005). The prevalence and parameters of personal therapy in the United States. In J. D. Geller, J. C. Norcross, & D. E. Orlinsky (Eds.), *The psychotherapist's own psychotherapy: Patient and clinician perspectives* (pp. 165–176). Oxford University Press.

Norcross, J. C., Lambert, M. J., & Wampold, B. E. (2019). *Psychotherapy relationships that work* (3rd ed.). Oxford University Press.

Orlinsky, D. E., & Ronnestad, M. H. (2005). *How psychotherapists develop: A study of therapeutic work and professional growth*. American Psychological Association.

Owen, J., & Hilsenroth, M. J. (2014). Treatment adherence: The importance of therapist flexibility in relation to therapy outcomes. *Journal of Counseling Psychology, 61*(2), 280–288. https://doi.org/10.1037/a0035753

Papathanasiou, I. V. (2015). Work-related mental consequences: Implications of burnout on mental health status among health care providers. *Acta Informatica Medica, 23*(1), 22–28. https://doi.org/10.5455/aim.2015.23.22-28

Parcover, J. A., & Swanson, J. L. (2013). Career counselor training and supervision: Role of the supervisory working alliance. *Journal of Employment Counseling, 50*(4), 166–178. https://doi.org/10.1002/j.2161-1920.2013.00035.x

Parsons, F. (1909). *Choosing a vocation*. Houghton Mifflin.

Perdrix, S., Stauffer, S., Masdonati, J., Massoudi, K., & Rossier, J. (2012). Effectiveness of career counseling: A one-year follow-up. *Journal of Vocational Behavior, 80*(2), 565–578. https://doi.org/10.1016/j.jvb.2011.08.011

Prescott, D. S., Maeschalck, C. L., & Miller, S. D. (Eds.). (2017). *Feedback-informed treatment in clinical practice: Reaching for excellence*. American Psychological Association. https://doi.org/10.1037/0000039-000

Prochaska, J. O., & DiClemente, C. C. (1983). Stages and processes of self-change of smoking: Toward an integrative model of change. *Journal of Consulting and Clinical Psychology, 51*(3), 390–395. https://doi.org/10.1037/0022-006X.51.3.390

Roche, M. K., Carr, A. L., Lee, I. H., Wen, J. H., & Brown, S. D. (2017). Career indecision in China: Measurement equivalence with the United States and South Korea. *Journal of Career Assessment, 25*(3), 526–536. https://doi.org/10.1177/1069072716651623

Rodolfa, E., Bent, R., Eisman, E., Nelson, P., Rehm, L., & Ritchie, P. (2005). A cube model for competency development: Implications for psychology educators and regulators. *Professional Psychology: Research and Practice, 36*(4), 347–354. https://doi.org/10.1037/0735-7028.36.4.347

Rousmaniere, T. (2016). *Deliberate practice for psychotherapists: A guide to improving clinical effectiveness*. Routledge. https://doi.org/10.4324/9781315472256

Rousmaniere, T. (2019). *Mastering the inner skills of psychotherapy: A deliberate practice manual*. Gold Lantern Books.

Rousmaniere, T., Goodyear, R., Miller, S. D., & Wampold, B. E. (Eds.). (2017). *The cycle of excellence: Using deliberate practice to improve supervision and training*. Wiley-Blackwell. https://doi.org/10.1002/9781119165590

Sampaio, C., Cardoso, P., Rossier, J., & Savickas, M. L. (2021). Attending to clients' psychological needs during career construction counseling. *The Career Development Quarterly, 69*(2), 96–113. https://doi.org/10.1002/cdq.12252

Santos, T. C., Mann, E. S., & Pfeffer, C. A. (2021). Are university health services meeting the needs of transgender college students? A qualitative assessment of a public university. *Journal of American College Health, 69*(1), 59–66. https://doi.org/10.1080/07448481.2019.1652181

Savickas, M. L., & Baker, D. B. (2005). The history of vocational psychology: Antecedents, origin, and early development. In W. B. Walsh & M. L. Savickas (Eds.), *Handbook of vocational psychology: Theory, research, and practice* (pp. 15–50). Lawrence Erlbaum Associates.

Sawant, N. S., Kamath, Y., Bajaj, U., Ajmera, K., & Lalwani, D. (2023). A study on impostor phenomenon, personality, and self-esteem of medical undergraduates and interns. *Industrial Psychiatry Journal, 32*(1), 136–141. https://doi.org/10.4103/ipj.ipj_59_22

Schlesinger, J., & Pasquarella Daley, L. (2016). Applying the chaos theory of careers as a framework for college career centers. *Journal of Employment Counseling, 53*(2), 86–96. https://doi.org/10.1002/joec.12030

Schultze, G., & Miller, C. M. (2004). The search for meaning and career development. *Career Development International, 9*(2), 142–152. https://doi.org/10.1108/13620430410526184

Schumacher, J. A., & Madson, A. B. (2014). *Fundamentals of motivational interviewing: Tips and strategies for addressing common clinical challenges.* Oxford University Press. https://doi.org/10.1093/med:psych/9780199354634.001.0001

Singh, A. A., & Moss, L. (2016). Using relational-cultural theory in LGBTQQ counseling: Addressing heterosexism and enhancing relational competencies. *Journal of Counseling & Development, 94*(4), 398–404. https://doi.org/10.1002/jcad.12098

Soares, J., Carvalho, C., & Silva, A. D. (2022). A systematic review on career interventions for university students: Framework, effectiveness, and outcomes. *Australian Journal of Career Development, 31*(2), 81–92. https://doi.org/10.1177/10384162221100460

Squire, L. R. (2004). Memory systems of the brain: A brief history and current perspective. *Neurobiology of Learning and Memory, 82*(3), 171–177. https://doi.org/10.1016/j.nlm.2004.06.005

Stiles, W. B., Honos-Webb, L., & Surko, M. (1998). Responsiveness in psychotherapy. *Clinical Psychology: Science and Practice, 5*(4), 439–458. https://doi.org/10.1111/j.1468-2850.1998.tb00166.x

Stiles, W. B., & Horvath, A. O. (2017). Appropriate responsiveness as a contribution to therapist effects. In L. G. Castonguay & C. E. Hill (Eds.), *How and why are some therapists better than others? Understanding therapist effects* (pp. 71–84). American Psychological Association. https://doi.org/10.1037/0000034-005

Storme, M., Celik, P., & Myszkowski, N. (2019). Career decision ambiguity tolerance and career decision-making difficulties in a French sample: The mediating role of career decision self-efficacy. *Journal of Career Assessment, 27*(2), 273–288. https://doi.org/10.1177/1069072717748958

Swanson, J. L., & Fouad, N. A. (2019). *Career theory and practice: Learning through case studies* (4th ed.). Sage Publications.

Taylor, J. M., & Neimeyer, G. J. (2017). The ongoing evolution of continuing education: Past, present, and future. In T. Rousmaniere, R. K. Goodyear, S. D. Miller, & B. E. Wampold (Eds.), *The cycle of excellence: Using deliberate practice to improve supervision and training* (pp. 219–248). Wiley-Blackwell.

Tracey, T. J. G., Wampold, B. E., Goodyear, R. K., & Lichtenberg, J. W. (2015). Improving expertise in psychotherapy. *Psychotherapy Bulletin, 50*(1), 7–13.

Udayar, S., Levin, N., Lipshits-Braziler, Y., Rochat, S., Di Fabio, A., Gati, I., Sovet, L., & Rossier, J. (2020). Difficulties in career decision making and self-evaluations: A meta-analysis. *Journal of Career Assessment, 28*(4), 608–635. https://doi.org/10.1177/1069072720910089

Uono, S., & Hietanen, J. K. (2015). Eye contact perception in the West and East: A cross-cultural study. *PLOS ONE, 10*(2), e0118094. https://doi.org/10.1371/journal.pone.0118094

U.S. Bureau of Labor Statistics. (2024, August 29). *Occupational outlook handbook.* https://www.bls.gov/ooh/

Ward, C. M., & Bingham, R. P. (1993). Career assessment of ethnic minority women. *Journal of Career Assessment, 1*(3), 246–257. https://doi.org/10.1177/106907279300100304

Wass, R., & Golding, C. (2014). Sharpening a tool for teaching: The zone of proximal development. *Teaching in Higher Education, 19*(6), 671–684. https://doi.org/10.1080/13562517.2014.901958

Whiston, S. C. (2020). Career counseling effectiveness and contributing factors. In P. J. Robertson, T. Hooley, & P. McCash (Eds.), *The Oxford handbook of career development* (pp. 337–352). Oxford University Press. https://doi.org/10.1093/oxfordhb/9780190069704.013.25

Whiston, S. C., Li, Y., Goodrich Mitts, N., & Wright, L. (2017). Effectiveness of career choice interventions: A meta-analytic replication and extension. *Journal of Vocational Behavior, 100*, 175–184. https://doi.org/10.1016/j.jvb.2017.03.010

Xu, H., & Bhang, C. H. (2019). The structure and measure of career indecision: A critical review. *The Career Development Quarterly, 67*(1), 2–20. https://doi.org/10.1002/cdq.12159

Zaretskii, V. (2009). The zone of proximal development: What Vygotsky did not have time to write. *Journal of Russian & East European Psychology, 47*(6), 70–93. https://doi.org/10.2753/RPO1061-0405470604

Index

A

Active effort, 168
Adjustments, of difficulty. *See* Difficulty assessments and adjustments
Ambivalence, client's. *See* Client ambivalence and skepticism
Annotated career counseling practice session transcript, 143–148
Assessment(s)
   of difficulty. *See* Difficulty assessments and adjustments
   feedback on career assessments, 93–105
   of trainee performance with real clients, 167
   underlying themes in. *See* Underlying themes in assessments

B

Benefits of career counseling, 69–78
   client statements for, 73–75
   counselor responses for, 76–78
   examples of, 71
   instructions for, 72
   skill criteria for, 70
   skill description for, 69–70
Body posture, 13
Breaks, taking, 169–170
Burned out client, 154–155

C

Career assessments, feedback on, 93–105
Career counseling
   benefits of. *See* Benefits of career counseling
   introduction to, 9–11
   role of deliberate practice in, 13–14
   trainee's work in, 171
Career counseling skills, 11
Career counseling style, personal, 163
Career indecision, 45
Client ambivalence and skepticism, 119–129
   client statements for, 124–126
   counselor responses for, 127–129
   examples of, 121–122
   instructions for, 123
   skill criteria for, 121
   skill description for, 119–121
Client outcomes, 170–171
Coker, Jerry, 8
Comfort, cultural, 10
Communication, nonverbal, 13, 170
Continual corrective feedback, 166
Cultural and familial influences, 57–66
   client statements for, 61–63
   counselor responses for, 64–66
   examples of, 58–59
   instructions for, 60
   skill criteria for, 58
   skill description for, 57–58
Culture, 10
Customization of exercises, 162–163
Cycle of deliberate practice, 7

D

Davis, Miles, 8
Decision-making styles, 45–54
   client statements for, 49–51
   counselor responses for, 52–54
   examples of, 46–47
   instructions for, 48
   skill criteria for, 46
   skill description for, 45–46
Declarative knowledge, 9
Deliberate practice
   cycle of, 7
   diary form, 179–180
   instructions for exercises, 17–19
   introduction to, 7–9
Difficulty assessments and adjustments, 153–154, 163, 165, 167, 175–177. *See also* Zone of proximal development

E

Effort, *vs.* flow, 168–169
Emotional stimuli, realistic, 161–162
Enmeshment, 9

Ericsson, K. Anders, 7
Eye contact, 13

F

Facial expressions, 13
Familial influences, client's. *See* Cultural and familial influences
Feedback, continual corrective, 166
Feedback on career assessments, 93–105
    client statements for, 97–99
    counselor responses for, 100–105
    examples of, 95
    instructions for, 96
    skill criteria for, 94
    skill description for, 93–94
Flow, 169
Fluency, verbal, 70

G

Gladwell, Malcolm, 7
Guidance for trainers and trainees, 161–172
    being mindful of trainee well-being, 164–165
    discover your own unique personal career counseling style, 163
    guidance for trainees, 168–172
    key points, 161–163
    respecting trainee privacy, 165
    responsive treatment, 164
    trainer self-evaluation, 165–168

H

Humility, cultural, 10

I

Identities, intersectional, 57–58
Improvisation, 8
Indecision, career, 45–46
Indecisive client, 156
Integration, of disparate pieces of training, 163–164
Intersectional identities, 57–58

J

Jazz analogy, 8

K

Knowledge, declarative *vs.* procedural, 9

L

Laid off client, 155–157
Learning exercises, simulation-based mastery, 8–9

M

Mastery learning exercises, simulation-based, 8–9
Mindfulness, of trainee well-being, 164–165
Mock career counseling sessions, 151–157
Monitoring of training results, 170
Multicultural orientation, 10
Music analogy, 8

N

Nonverbal communication, 13, 170

O

Observation of trainee's work performance, 166
Opportunities, cultural, 10

Outcome measurements, 170–171
Outliers (Gladwell), 7

P

Paraphrasing, 24, 58
Parsons, Frank, 10
Personal development, trainee's, 171
Personal style, discovering, 163
Playfulness, 169–170
Posture, 13
Practice session transcript, 143–148
Privacy, of trainee, 165

R

Reaction toward trainer, complex, 171–172
Realistic emotional stimuli, 161–162
Rehearsal, 163
Respecting trainee privacy, 165
Responsive treatment, 164
Role-playing, 151–152

S

Sample career counseling syllabus, 183–192
Sarcastic client, 155–156
Self-efficacy, 165
Self-evaluation, trainer's, 165–168
Session goals. *See* Setting session goals
Setting session goals, 81–91
    client statements for, 86–88
    counselor responses for, 89–91
    examples of, 83–84
    instructions for, 85
    skill criteria for, 83
    skill description for, 81–83
Simulation-based mastery learning exercises, 8–9
Skepticism, client's. *See* Client ambivalence and skepticism
Skills, 23–32
    client statements for, 27–29
    counselor responses for, 30–32
    examples of, 24–25
    instructions for, 26
    skill criteria for, 24
Speech pacing, 170
State-dependent learning, 8–9
Supervisors, 164
Support, of career counselors, 10

T

"10,000-hour rule," 7–8
Tone of voice, 13, 170
Trainees. *See also* Guidance for trainers and trainees
    alliance with trainer, 171–172
    own therapy, 172
    performance with real clients, 167
    personal development, 171
    privacy, 165
    training process, 171
    well-being, 164–165
Trainer self-evaluation, 165–168
Trainer-trainee alliance, 171–172
Training results, monitoring of, 170
Transcript, practice session, 143–148

U

Underlying themes in assessments, 107–116
    client contexts for, 111–113
    counselor responses for, 114–116

examples of, 108–109
instructions for, 110
skill criteria for, 108
skill description for, 107–108

V

Values, 35–43
client statements for, 38–40
counselor responses for, 41–43
examples of, 36
instructions for, 37
skill criteria for, 36
skill description for, 35–36
Verbal fluency, 70
Vocal tone, 13, 170

W

Well-being, of trainees, 164–165
Whiston, S. C., 10

Z

Zone of proximal development, 166–168

About the Authors

Jennifer M. Taylor, PhD, is the senior director of the American Psychological Association's (APA's) Office of Continuing Education Sponsor Approval and is a former associate professor of counseling psychology at the University of Utah and a former assistant professor at West Virginia University, where she spent a decade teaching courses on career and vocational counseling. Dr. Taylor also taught as an instructor at the University of Florida in courses spanning theories in counseling to psychological disorders and diagnoses. She is the author of nearly 50 peer-reviewed journal articles, books, and book chapters and 70 national, regional, and invited presentations on enhancing professional competence and personal well-being and best practices in education and lifelong learning for professional psychologists. Her clinical work spans working at three large university counseling centers, one multicultural community college student center, a university career counseling center consistently ranked as a top career counseling center in the nation, a psychiatric hospital, and a nonprofit counseling center for low-income women and children. Dr. Taylor is the recipient of several teaching awards, including the University of Utah College of Education Early Career Teaching Award, the University of Utah Daniels Fund Ethics Initiative Leadership in Ethics Education Award, the APA Board of Educational Affairs Cynthia D. Belar Education Advocacy Distinguished Service Award, the University of Florida University-Wide Graduate Student Teaching Award, and the Pearson Education Outstanding Graduate Student Teaching Award. Dr. Taylor is passionate about social justice and advocacy and served as the tri-chair for the APA Division 17 Presidential Initiative on Engaging Advocacy in Counseling Psychology; the chair of the APA's Board of Educational Affairs, a Working Group Member for the APA's Presidential Initiative on Citizen Psychologists; co-chair of APA's Society of Counseling Psychology Response Working Group on Anti-Racist and Anti-Sexist Education; vice chair and chair of APA's Continuing Education Committee; and a taskforce leader for APA's Society of Counseling Psychology Advancement of Women HERstory.

Alexandre Vaz, PhD, is cofounder and chief academic officer of Sentio University and the Sentio Counseling Center. He provides workshops, webinars, and advanced clinical training and supervision to clinicians around the world. Dr. Vaz is the author or coeditor of many books on deliberate practice and psychotherapy training. He has held multiple committee roles for the Society for the Exploration of Psychotherapy Integration and the Society for Psychotherapy Research. Dr. Vaz is founder and host of *Psychotherapy Expert Talks*, an acclaimed interview series with distinguished psychotherapists and therapy researchers.

Tony Rousmaniere, PsyD, is cofounder and program director of Sentio University and the Sentio Counseling Center. He provides workshops, webinars, and advanced clinical training and supervision to clinicians around the world. Dr. Rousmaniere is the author or coeditor of many books on deliberate practice and psychotherapy training. In 2017, he published the widely cited article "What Your Therapist Doesn't Know" in *The Atlantic*. Dr. Rousmaniere supports the open-data movement and publishes his aggregated clinical outcome data, in deidentified form, on his website (https://www.drtonyr.com). Dr. Rousmaniere is president of Division 29 (Society for the Advancement of Psychotherapy) of the American Psychological Association.